To Him
who by means of his power
working in us
is able to do
so much more
than we can ever ask for,
or even think of:

to God be the glory
in the church
and in Christ Jesus
for all time,
for ever and ever!

British Library Cataloguing in Publication Data

Long, Graham
    Thank God you've come: a guide for those seeking to offer more
    effective pastoral care
    1. Christian Church. Pastoral work
    I. Title

ISBN 0 9519 4550 5

First published in 1992 by the Wessex Province of the United Reformed Church,
King's Road, Chandler's Ford, Eastleigh, Hampshire, SO5 2EY.

Second Edition published in 1996 by the United Reformed Church House,
86 Tavistock Place, London WC1H 9RT

ACKNOWLEDGEMENTS

The Collect for Purity and other extracts from the *Alternative Service Book* © 1980 are
reprinted by permission of the Central Board of Finance of the Church of England.

The Statement from the Methodist Covenant Service is copyright © The Methodist
Conference 1975 and is used by permission of the Methodist Publishing House.

Contents

In affectionate memory of the two Almas

whose pastoral wisdom and practical care

gave such enthusiastic support

to the writing of this book

and who, sadly, died before it was published.

FOREWORD

The eldership is one of the greatest resources possessed by the United Reformed Church. It is one of the greatest riches in its own life. It is one of the greatest contributions which it has to share with other denominations in the ecumenical movement generally and at grass root level in local ecumenical projects.

Sadly, it is a resource which has not always been used as fully as it might. In some congregations, elders have not yet caught the vision of what the leadership role of the elder might be. In others, the elder's function is very little different from that of a Deacon in the former Congregational church. Elsewhere elders may have embarked on their duties, unsure of their role, daunted particularly by the thought of undertaking responsibility of a pastoral nature.

This book aims to redress this and to develop the full potential of the eldership, particularly in its pastoral care. It is, in fact, a manual of pastoral care, full of practical advice to elders, both those taking up their duties for the first time and those who may have served for more years than they like to remember.

The emphasis throughout is on the elder as a person called to share in the pastoral care of members, rather than just to be a member of a committee. It deals in a practical way with practical matters: priorities, techniques of visiting, praying with and for people, elders' groups, dealing with the lapsed. It does so with thoroughness and sensitivity and is biblically based throughout. If the advice given here is acted on, it will improve beyond measure the pastoral care given by elders and their like.

The book is born out of the experience of a discerning minister, skilled in training others and equipping them for their work. It has grown through ministry in places as different as the Channel Islands and the Surrey commuter belt. It reflects recent experience in the wider context of a newly established Methodist/URC congregation. Some of the material has been used with great appreciation in elders' training within the Guildford District of the United Reformed Church. When, because of this, it came to the attention of the Faith and Life Department of the Wessex Province, as part of its concern for eldership training, the Department felt that it deserved a much wider clientele and encouraged Graham to make it available more generally.

I have great pleasure in commending this book to a wide circle. I believe that elders need help if they are to carry out their duties and responsibilities to the best of their ability. This book will be of immense value to newly-ordained elders starting out on their work and undertaking pastoral visiting for the first time. It will enable those with years of service behind them to carry out their pastoral responsibility in a more satisfying and caring way. Nor is its value by any means limited to the United Reformed Church. Here is a manual which anyone charged with responsibility for pastoral care, in any denomination, will find immensely helpful. I am sure that all who read it will be enabled to offer more effective pastoral care to the people of God.

Nelson W Bainbridge

Moderator
Wessex Province
United Reformed Church

PREFACE

"Thank God you've come!" she said, plainly having been in tears before coming to the door. "Everything's going wrong! I just don't know what to do; I'm at my wit's end. I was so hoping you'd call." Her surprise at seeing him on the doorstep was matched by his amazement at her welcome. He'd actually set out to visit someone else on his care list but found his thoughts constantly turning to her. So he'd changed his plans and had gone to see her instead. As he talked about this experience he echoed her welcome: "Thank God I went!"

That incident stands in sharp contrast to another. He came to the manse to see me. "You've got to do something about Dad," he said. "Mum's at her wit's end. He's so bad tempered these days. The garden's going to rack and ruin and the neighbours are complaining about the weeds. And he's never got the time to talk to my sister and me. He's always busy doing something for the Church!"

I was glad he'd come to share the family's distress with me. I spent some time listing all the things the boy's father had been asked to do or had volunteered to do. Then I added all the other jobs he'd never been asked to do, never volunteered to do, but nonetheless somehow accumulated over the years. The total was formidable and provided the basis for a much needed review of the father's over-commitment to his church.

Incidents like that form one part of the background to the chapters that follow. They raise important issues about the ways we help one another, as elders and leaders in local churches, to assess our priorities and allocate our time. Some of the chapters in this book seek to address these issues.

Other themes first arose out of a quite different need. The formation of the United Reformed Church in 1972 proved a time of crisis for many of the leaders in former Congregational Churches. It was one thing to agree to the transition from deacon to elder as a matter of policy within the national Scheme of Union with the Presbyterians from whom the eldership was gained. It was quite another to come to an Elders' Meeting shortly afterwards and meet the personal challenge to accept pastoral responsibility for a group of members.

Some of the chapters that follow first began to form in response to that need. Some of them were produced in the Channel Islands as back-up papers for elders' retreat and training days. Others were drafted to deal with particular situations where elders were feeling the strains of their ministry.

The publication in 1984 of a book of vestry and communion prayers written by the elders of Camberley United Reformed Church under the title "*Prayers of a Year*" brought a flood of letters from all over the country. Many contained personal accounts of the difficulties elders experienced when they came to this ministry and showed a great need for practical help and encouragement.

The passing years have done little to diminish the need to encourage and support our elders. But there has been little available to which reference can be made for the practical tools of pastoral care. There is also a continuing need to assist new elders in the simplest form possible so that they can quickly gain some satisfaction in their service.

ACKNOWLEDGEMENTS

I am immensely grateful to the elders of Camberley United Reformed Church who encouraged me to continue to develop such aides. I am particularly grateful to the Elders' Training Group of the Guildford District of the United Reformed Church for an invitation to lead a District Elders' Training Day in 1988. For this it was necessary to expand the material I had already accumulated. The response of the elders present suggested real need. "Why wasn't I given help like this years ago?" was the frequent question.

A request from the Faith and Life Committee of the URC's Wessex Province to make the material more widely available was overtaken by the need to train a new generation of elders on the formation in Camberley of the Church of High Cross as a United Reformed and Methodist Church in 1990. Additional chapters have been added which take up some of the questions that have arisen in the months since.

In all that follows I cannot emphasise too strongly that the pastoral care of the elder is to be seen in the setting of the full ministry of the church, a crucial part of which is as minister and elders share together. If, in writing specifically to the ministry of the elder, this proper setting is not always made explicit, I hope that nonetheless what is written will be read in that context.

I am most grateful for the encouragement and support of the Revd Nelson Bainbridge, Moderator of the Wessex Province, who has kindly contributed the Foreword. I am indebted also to Sue Hitchins for her comments on the text of Our Ministry to Children, to Christine Hardwick who assisted with the index, to David Buckingham of Artworks, Camberley, who created the cover design (updated 1996), and to David Page for his meticulous yet gracious work as editor.

Finally, the writing of this book has occupied many hours at the desk and even more in reflection as the chapters have been worked out in my mind. The whole exercise has been a salutary reminder of the need to plan carefully if the needs of one's own family are properly to be met. Lessons are learned as much through failure as by success and words of appreciation are insufficient to convey the debt of gratitude I owe to my wife, Sheila, for her unfailing forbearance throughout the many months this book has preoccupied my thoughts. Without her pastoral care working quietly within the manse itself the task would not have been completed.

While these chapters have been written against the background of the United Reformed Church, I hope that they will prove of help to any called to pastoral care and leadership in the local church. I am grateful to the many elders and other folk who have so freely shared their thoughts and feelings about their own ministries. I hope I have heard aright what they have said to me and that what follows will be of value. If, however, it misses the mark, the responsibility is mine alone. Hopefully, the conversation will go on.

Graham Long
Camberley

CARING PROPERLY FOR OURSELVES

A careful regard for our own needs

is but prudent if we seek the

whole-hearted care of others.

Our calling as elders

The work of elders and ministers is determined by our understanding of the church. Though the calling and setting apart of elders has a long and honourable tradition, and though the eldership is a feature of many different churches across the world, there are variations in the way the work of an elder is worked out in practice. But, in every instance, it has been worked out as an expression of the particular church's understanding of its nature and purpose.

It sometimes comes as a surprise to our elders to discover that the United Reformed Church has a clearly stated purpose. This is set out in *The Manual* of the United Reformed Church in *The Basis of Union* and is reprinted below in the revised form agreed at the 1990 General Assembly.

The purpose of the Church

"Within the one, holy, catholic, apostolic Church the United Reformed Church acknowledges its responsibility under God:

♦ to make its life a continual offering of itself and the world to God in adoration and worship through Jesus Christ;

♦ to receive and express the renewing life of the Holy Spirit in each place and in its total fellowship, and there to declare the reconciling and saving power of the life, death and resurrection of Jesus Christ;

♦ to live out, in joyful and sacrificial service to all in their various physical and spiritual needs, that ministry of caring, forgiving and healing love which Jesus Christ brought to all whom he met;

♦ to bear witness to Christ's rule over the nations in all the variety of their organized life."

(The Basis of Union, paragraph 11)

This statement makes a starting point for thinking about the life and work of the church. The church needs various ministries to accomplish its purpose and, as part of these, elders share with the minister in the pastoral oversight and leadership of the local church. Normally each elder is entrusted with the care of a group of members and pastoral care is usually a feature within the agenda of the Elders' Meeting.

The task of elders and ministers is to carry forward the purpose of the church. Our work, therefore, is concerned essentially with worship, with renewal, with care and with mission. It is these overall concerns that are worked out as practical tasks in some detail in *The Manual* of the United Reformed Church in paragraph 2(2) of *The Structure of the United Reformed Church.*

Before looking in some depth at ways we can organize and equip ourselves for the pastoral aspect of our work as elders, it is worth looking afresh at the practical tasks set out in the *The Manual.* They are reprinted below with a number of key words highlighted. These key words give the clue to the overall character of the ministry of the elder.

The function of the Elders' Meeting

The Elders' Meeting of the local church consists of the minister and elders elected by church meeting and is charged with the spiritual oversight of the local church. Its functions are set out as follows:

(i)   to **foster** in the congregation concern for witness and service to the community, evangelism at home and abroad, Christian education, ecumenical action, local inter-church relations and the wider responsibilities of the whole church;

(ii)   to **see** that public worship is regularly offered and the sacraments duly administered, and generally to **promote** the welfare of the congregation;

(iii)   to **ensure** pastoral care of the congregation, in which the minister is joined by elders having particular responsibility for groups of members;

(iv)   to **nominate** from among its members a church secretary (or secretaries), to be elected by the church meeting, to serve both the church meeting and the Elders' Meeting;

(v)   to **arrange** for pulpit supply in a vacancy;

(vi)   to **keep** the roll of members and (as an aid to the discharge of the congregation's pastoral and evangelistic responsibility) lists of names of adherents and children attached to the congregation, and in consultation with the church meeting to **maintain** standards of membership and to **advise** on the admission of members on profession of faith and by transfer, on the suspension of members, and on the removal of names from the roll;

(vii)   to **be responsible** for the institution and oversight of work among children and young people and of all organisations within the congregation;

(viii)   to **call** for the election of elders and **advise** on the number required;

(ix)   to **consider** the suitability of applicants for recognition as a candidate for the ministry (including the non-stipendiary ministry) and to **advise** church meeting about its recommendation to the district council;

(x)   to **recommend** to the church meeting arrangements for the proper maintenance of buildings and the general oversight of all the financial responsibilities of the local church;

(xi)   to **act** on behalf of the church meeting and **bring** concerns to the wider councils of the United Reformed Church;

(xii)   to **do** such other things as may be necessary in pursuance of its responsibility for the common life of the church.

(The Structure of the United Reformed Church, paragraph 2(2))

With one exception, the highlighted words are all active verbs. They make it very clear that the elders are not expected themselves to shoulder all the active work of the church. Rather, it is the responsibility of the elders to get other people dynamically involved. Many of the verbs make it plain that the key concept in all this is **encouragement**.

The task of the elder may be summarised well in the three words "ministry of encouragement". *The Manual* does not, however, explain how we relate this to the individual for whom we accept a pastoral care responsibility. To what ends do we exercise a pastoral ministry of encouragement?

Our ministry of encouragement

What are we to encourage? Nowhere is this spelt out in precise detail, but the New Testament does give more than enough clues for us to get a clear picture.

We are to encourage our people

to be what they are: The summons to be what we are is an urgent note in the writings of the apostles. Peter expresses it well when he writes "you are the chosen race, the King's priests, the holy nation, God's own people, chosen to proclaim the wonderful acts of God, who called you out of darkness into his own marvellous light. At one time you were not God's people, but now you are his people; at one time you did not know God's mercy, but now you have received his mercy." *(1 Peter 2:9-10)*. Though we may need to do a cultural exchange in working Peter's words out in the contemporary world, clearly our task is to encourage our people to be what they are - the people of God.

to spiritual liveliness: Paul's encouragement to the church members in Ephesus *(Ephesians 5:19)* to "speak to one another with words of psalms, hymns, and sacred songs" and to "sing hymns and psalms to the Lord" with praise in their hearts, speaks of a sharing relationship which is far from the ordinary and general. It is a relationship "in Christ" and a reminder to us that we are given the Holy Spirit to take away our timidity and fill us with power, love and self-control *(2 Timothy 1:7)*.

to moral improvement: Our hearts and minds are to be "set on the things that are in heaven", says Paul before going on to speak of moral matters. This teaching features strongly throughout Paul's letters. First he writes of the Good News in a rich variety of ways, then he presents the challenge to moral improvement which reflects and effects that Good News *(Colossians 3)*. Some people accomplish much through great personal ambition and the driving force of an iron will. Most of us are not in their class. We need a great deal of encouragement to show any sign of improvement in quite humdrum things. We need even more if we are to show real growth of moral stature and Christ-like behaviour.

to self-effacing witness: Jesus commands public witness so that God may receive the glory. He said "your light must shine before people, so that they will see the good things you do and praise your Father in heaven" *(Matthew 5:16)*. This is so central to God's purposes, that in the great picture of the outcome of mission in Revelation 7, all attention is focused on God. It's so easy to do what people say is the right thing and to find ourselves the centre of attention. We need encouragement and practical help if we are to be self-effacing in the right way, the way that points to the love of a heavenly Father who is the source of all goodness.

As elders we have a role which is critical in the divine purpose. It is God's purpose that **"we shall all grow up in every way to Christ"** *(Ephesians 4:15)*. It is God's purpose, to put it another way, to see that **"Christ's nature is formed in us"** *(Galatians 4:19)*.

Our task is to encourage what God is doing in all our people's lives. Without doubt, we shall only succeed when we are open to the work of God in our own lives, and thirsting for it to be brought to a marvellous completion - to his glory and praise *(Philippians 1:6 and 9-11)*.

"**G**iven the time . . ."

One of the most common problems confronting anyone who is asked to take on voluntary work of any kind is finding the time to do it. Frequently we say, "Given the time, I'd love to" This is true in the life of the church also. Yet time and again we hear people say of others "I don't know how they find the time to do it all". And that gives us the clue. The time is there. All we have to do is to find it!

The calling of anyone to Christian service through the life of the church carries with it one fundamental assumption. If we do not grasp the truth of that assumption very firmly, we shall find that things begin to go wrong.

Time

When God calls on anyone to serve him, he **always** provides the time in which it is to be done.

That doesn't mean that we shan't have a lot of sorting out to do. Finding the time is seldom easy. Yet we can begin that search with a quiet confidence that (a) the time is there, (b) God wants us to find it, and (c) he doesn't expect us to find it out of our own resources; he expects us to seek his help in finding it. All time is given but none more so than the time to be used in response to God's calling to a particular task.

But that raises a question about our calling. How can we be sure that God is calling us to do something special for him?

A matter of calling

The question of calling has two parts to it: being sure that we are called and finding the time to meet the call.

Being sure that we are called

If our churches are careful how elders are selected we may be fairly confident that the church's calling is God's calling. We must not let ourselves be deceived by giving undue importance either to our own feelings or to what we see others doing. The most common feeling expressed throughout the Bible by those God calls to serve him is one of utter astonishment. "Who am I, Lord, that you should ask me . . . " is the most common response.

In addition, we often reflect worldly standards of judgement when considering what is useful. Yet, throughout the Bible, the people God calls to serve him are the ones that worldly judgement has dismissed as of no account. Most of all this is true of Jesus himself.

We need, therefore, to see our inadequacies in the light of the Bible's teaching about God's ways. God takes us on with all our weaknesses. He doesn't ask that we perfect ourselves before he can call us into his service. He knows we can't do that. So he takes us as we are, simply asking us to be open to the Holy Spirit so that he can work through us. When the church has carefully sought the guidance of the Holy Spirit before inviting us to take up a particular work of ministry we may be fairly confident, astonishing as it may seem, that God is calling us to serve him in that way.

Finding the time to meet the calling

Once we have accepted that God provides the time along with the calling, it becomes as much a matter of organization as of anything else. How do we organize our time? How do we establish our priorities?

We can, of course, ask other elders who are more experienced how they have set about organizing their time. Alternatively, the pattern on the next page may help us to identify certain thing very quickly. There will be some activities which can simply be ignored or with which we may become involved only once in every several years. But there are some which will be monthly requirements, some quarterly or annually, some within a periodic rota, and some which will be of weekly or even daily concern. So it is possible for us to get a clear idea of the range of things with which we are involved.

The range of activities of an elder are summarised in the following table:

MEETINGS	within the local church	Elders' meetings
		Church meetings
		Group meetings
		Committees
		Organizations
	in the denomination [1]	District Council [1]
		Provincial Synod [1]
		Committees [1]
		General Assembly [1]
VISITING	members of your group	Formal visits
		Informal visits
		Social visits
	those assisting you [1]	'Information' contact [2]
		'Support' contact [2,3]
PERSONAL SUPPORT		Elders' communion [3]
		Pastoral worker [3]
		Minister
		Retreats
		Training days
		Quiet days
		Courses
MINISTRY	within the local church	Communion Elder
		Vestry prayer

Notes:

1. Not all elders are involved in wider representative activities but the possibility of these needs to be taken into account.

2. 'Information' contact is the time needed to keep any helpers you have fully informed, so that they can assist you effectively. 'Support' contact is the time you must allocate to caring for them as people, taking a personal interest in them and giving them encouragement.

3.　　Not all churches have these support structures but the time required for them needs to be included when assessing priorities.

Estimating our time

But how much time to allow? Each of us must look very hard at the total demands on our time. Our service as an elder is not the only priority we have, but we may well need to check whether all the things we now count as priorities really are. It is likely that we will have some things in our timetable that we very much enjoy doing but which may not in fact really be priorities. Because they are so enjoyable it may be difficult to give them up and we may need help in sorting things out.

Chart 1 on the next page, therefore, suggests a way to work out the time we need to allocate. For some this way of approaching things may seem too mechanistic but it has proved helpful to others and may in any case provide a useful periodic check to see whether we are actually giving our families a fair deal.

Chart 1 may also prove valuable in assessing the balance in our ministry. It can help us to see whether the burden of our ministry is in attending meetings or directly with the people for whom we have to care. For some the executive function within the elder's role becomes the dominant part of the work. Sharing in the decision making processes of the church at a critical point gathers greater significance than the pastoral care of our people. To recognise this is not to say that the executive function is unimportant or to demean the conscientious way that elders seek to provide pastoral care. But it is to admit that for many of us it is easier to put another meeting into our diaries than to offer an apology for absence because we have already allotted that time to visit our people. We need to keep a balance.

The truth is that sometimes the decisions we have to make in Elders' Meeting would be more soundly based if we had a greater awareness of the thoughts and feelings of our people. This may suggest that the attention of many of us should be directed more to the pastoral aspect of our role.

Use **Chart 1** as an aid to calculate how much time you will need. Think of a morning, an afternoon or an evening as one unit of time. Then if, for example, you decide to give the equivalent of one day a week except during holiday time, you would have (52-4)"x"3 = 144 units of time available per year.

Meetings							
	Elders	(?)	11	x	1	=	11
	Church meeting	(?)	9	x	1	=	9
	Group meetings			x	1	=	
	Committees			x	1	=	
	Organizations			x	1	=	

Total time within my own church   =

District Council	4	x	1	=	4
Provincial Synod	2	x	2	=	4
Committees		x	1	=	
Consultations		x	1	=	
General Assembly	5	x	3	=	15
Other representation		x		=	

Total time within wider church   =

Visiting				
	Formal visits	x	=	
	Informal visits	x	=	
	Social visits	x	=	

Total time visiting my group   =

'Information' contact	x	=	
'Support' contact	x	=	

Total time supporting my helpers   =

Personal support:

Elders' communion	x	=	
Minister/Pastoral worker	x	=	
Retreats	x	=	
Training days	x	=	
Quiet days	x	=	
Courses	x	=	

Total time receiving personal support   =

Ministry within local church:

Communion Elder	x	=	
Vestry prayer	x	=	

Total time preparing to share in ministry   =

Estimated total time requirements in units   =

Chart 1. Estimating our time

Assessing our priorities

Clearly the proper care of one's spouse and family is a priority. This is so important that it could helpfully be part of the understanding implicit in the calling of every elder. We need to talk through the time demands with our spouse, and children where appropriate, and to reach an agreement with them, allowing for some flexibility which we will try not to abuse. This is just as important in the case of single elders who need to look after the best interests of their wider families.

Chart 2 on the next page may be of some help in making any adjustments that are needed following such consideration of priorities. We may assume that elders are people of good conscience who will not wish to let others down. So it is not easy to adjust our priorities at the drop of a hat. We need to think through the effect this will have on others and what we will need to do to make any changes with as little disruption for them as possible. But it is at this point in our thinking that we often begin to feel very guilty and sometimes the reactions of others involved compound this feeling. We're made to feel that we are letting them down.

So we need to remember another golden rule:

┌─ **Our successor** ─────────────────────────────────

When God asks us to do something different for him, he already knows who will take on the jobs we have to give up and he will make his choice plain when the time is right.

A number of things follow from this rule.

♦ We mustn't be deterred by the insidious thought that we can't see who our successor is to be. It really doesn't matter that we don't know who will take on the job.

♦ We mustn't be fooled by the misconception that because we have done a job for several years a vacancy would be disastrous. It may well be the case, as sometimes it is when a minister moves, that the church needs space before being ready to receive God's replacement.

♦ We mustn't be misled by any suggestion that it is up to us to find someone to do the work needed. It is the church's proper responsibility, however uncomfortable that may make things for others.

When we respond positively to the call of God to adjust our priorities, we should try to let go with a peaceful heart and mind - whatever other people might say.

Use **Chart 2** to plan your priorities and needs. First list your major activities, both those that are not related to your work as an elder and those that are or will be related to your work. From this list pick the four or five items which have top

---

What active rôles do I have in the life of my church?

(a) Not directly related to my work as an elder?

Priority
Give up
Need help

(b) Directly related to my work as an elder?

what steps must I take to give up each activity noted?

What steps must I take to obtain the support I need?

Chart 2. Sorting out your priorities

priority and mark them in the first column on the right. In the second column place a mark by those activities which you will have to give up, and in the last column place a mark by those activities for which you will need additional support. Finally, at the bottom of the chart make lists of the steps you will have to take to give up the activities you have marked and to get the support you will need.

Keeping up the good work

We've already noted that God doesn't want us to find the time out of our own resources. Nor does he expect us to fulfil our responsibilities as elders solely through our personal gifts and strengths. Of course, we all have particular talents we can bring to the ministry of the elder and we are not expected to let these wither away by neglecting to use them. But there is very much that we require as elders that we cannot supply from our own resources, however well trained we may be in the art of personal relationships or well-tutored in the skills of compassion.

There is much that we can have only as a gift from the God who has called us to serve him. And that means our greatest need is to stay in lively communion with him and in fellowship with one another. The diagram on the next page indicates some of the ways of achieving this that a considerate church may provide for its elders. Hopefully, some will offer additional ways not included here but it is more likely that only some of them will be found in the programme of any one local church. This diagram gives us a chance to see where we may find springs of refreshment or the support and encouragement of others. It can also help us to see how we belong together as a "fellowship of carers at the heart of the life of the church".

Not all churches will be able to provide so many channels of care and support but all of us exercising a ministry in the local church should be able to use the overall framework and to identify within it the care and support we do receive. Many of the categories of care and support are not mutually exclusive and many inter-relate. The framework should help us to see whether we are receiving the support needed to sustain, and to fulfil, the ministry to which the church has called us.

Sources of support

Shared responsibility   Minister and church secretary
(Elders' meeting)

Elder's group informal
Pastoral worker   relationships

Befrienders within   Support from non-serving
the elder's group   T A S K   elders

· · · · · · · · · ·   · · · · · · · · · ·

        S U P P O R T

Concern of the   ·   · Shared "know-how" of
minister   T   other elders
       F   R

       A   C   The care   A
Care within the   M   A   I   District elders'
church as in any   I   R   of our   N   training programme
other household   L   E   I
       Y   elders   N   Local church retreat
Concern of church   G   days
secretary   ·

     ·   P E R S O N A L   · Province quiet days

· · · · · · · · · ·   · · · · · · · · · ·

       S U P P O R T
Elder's family   Pastoral worker

Elder's communion   From other elders

Personal devotions   Prayers of other people

From minister and   Back-up from non-serving
church officers   elders

The elder's circle of care

We see from the diagram above that every elder is surrounded by a 'circle of care'. Use the chart on the next page to analyse your own circle of care. Beside each number, put on the inside your personal needs and on the outside the names of those whose help is required if your need is to be met.

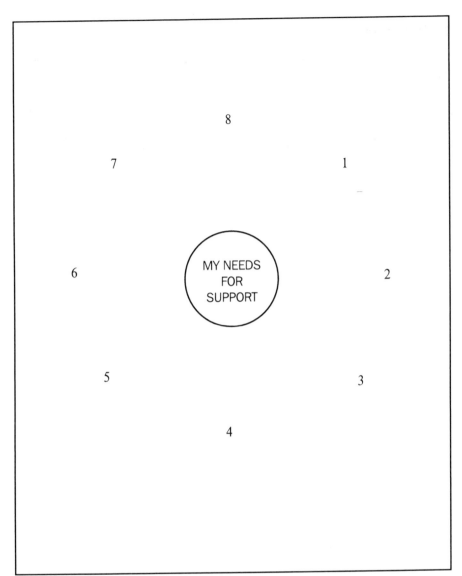

8

7

1

MY NEEDS
FOR
SUPPORT

6

2

5

3

4

Chart 3. Your circle of care

Once you have identified what your needs are don't be afraid to ask others for their help. Our fellow church members want us to succeed in the tasks to which they have called us. Don't struggle on in mounting personal distress. Ask for the help you need.

Satisfaction

When assessing our priorities and allocating our time there is one final thing to remember:

Satisfaction

The satisfaction gained from responding willingly to God's call will far exceed the pleasure we fear we may lose through giving up the things we now so much enjoy.

CARING PASTORALLY FOR OUR PEOPLE

The whole-hearted care of others is more than a practice or a programme. It flows as they are held in proper regard, and is best conducted with the expectation of mutual enrichment as the initial, often hesitant, relationship is made glorious as giver and receiver in their turn become receiver and giver.

Pastoral care

The Statement on Ministry in *The Basis of Union* of the United Reformed Church says that "Elders share with ministers of the word and sacraments in the pastoral oversight and leadership of the local churches" (*The Basis of Union*, paragraph 22).

In consequence one vital function of the Elders' Meeting is to ensure the pastoral care of the congregation. In this ministers and elders join together. Nowhere, however, does the Statement explain what it means by the terms it uses, such as "pastoral oversight and leadership". It seems to assume that we shall all know enough about pastoral matters to be able to give the leadership allotted to us.

There are signs that churches are thinking for themselves. For instance, although the Statement says that each elder will have particular responsibility for a group of members, variations within this practice are being explored by some churches. Such thinking, however, is to do with structures for pastoral care rather than the nature of pastoral care itself. For many the basic question remains. What is it that we are trying to do when we set out to care pastorally for people?

What is pastoral care

Many different approaches can be taken in answer to this question. Some pick up on the extensive pastoral background in the Bible and explore the title used by Jesus - The Good Shepherd. One highly commended example of this is Bishop Lesslie Newbigin's most helpful book of short addresses first given to parish leaders in South India, and published under the title *"The Good Shepherd"*.

An alternative approach recalls that Christians are people of the **new** commandment. To the ten commandments of the Old Covenant, Jesus added one in his own name: "I give you a new commandment: love one another. As I have loved you, so you must love one another." That was the instruction he gave to his disciples immediately after he had washed their feet *(John 13:34)*. Christian pastoral care is simply the application of that new commandment through the life of the church.

Two things follow from this.

1.   We look to Jesus to define the objectives and the manner of our pastoral care. Its inspiration lies in the words "as I have loved you": its genius in our ability to embody those words in the life of the church.

2.   Just as the Ten Commandments were given to define the character of God's people in a manner which reflected the freedom God had granted them from bondage in Egypt, so the new commandment given by Jesus is to define the character of the fellowship of his followers, the church. "If you have love for one another, then everyone will know that you are my disciples" *(John 13:35)*. So care for one another within the church is not an optional extra or a secondary matter. It belongs to the essential nature of the true church.

While the application of the new commandment primarily is to be within the fellowship, inevitably it spills over into the surrounding community.

It is the responsibility of ministers and elders working together to ensure the pastoral care of the congregation - that is, to foster 'love for one another' within the fellowship.

Pastoral care in the local church

There is no universally set pattern of pastoral care. What is suitable for a fast growing suburban congregation may not work in a small village church. What is useful where there is a full-time resident minister may be less helpful in a group pastorate. What works where there are elders who are long-term residents in the community may meet difficulties in a commuter-belt fellowship with frequent changes of leadership.

The genius of pastoral care is therefore to work out together the pattern best for the local situation. It may prove helpful to bear the following points in mind when doing so.

1.   Pastoral care does not equal visiting. Visiting is part of pastoral care but is not an end in itself. Some approaches to visiting are simply a waste of time. Others can be like gold-dust. When properly conducted, visiting is a valuable arm of pastoral care, but pastoral care that is merely limited to visiting is a poor thing indeed. More will be said about 'visiting' in due course.

2.   There are four things - all of which will be dealt with at greater length - which are properly part of pastoral care:

Prayer
Visiting
Giving
Receiving

The ministry of Jesus contains many examples of these basic pastoral activities. A careful study of them linked with the letters of the New Testament - quite often the second half of the letter - should produce more than enough inspiration and know-how to develop pastoral care; sufficient, that is, to enable even the most hesitant among us to begin to make an effective contribution to the pastoral care of the church.

3.   While pastoral care needs to be shaped carefully to meet the particular needs of the local church, it is important not to forget the informal and often spontaneous caring that goes on in every community. A full understanding of the elders' work of pastoral care will include encouraging this informal caring within the congregation.

The ancient world marvelled at the early Church not because the Church was good at organizing but because Christians were good at caring. It said: "How these Christians love one another".

The three "C"s of pastoral care

Received as a particular treasure of the Presbyterian tradition, the caring rôle of the elders is still being explored in many churches. As a concept it still meets with opposition from those who assert that "all this is ministers' work". But appreciation of its value is fast growing.

Whatever structure is used locally to carry the pastoral care of the congregation, pastoral care will contain a three-fold emphasis:

Care: love showing itself in action; that is, true love. The evangelist John says "we love because God first loved us". Pastoral care is both a response to that love on our part as carers and also the offering of ourselves and our actions as instruments for God's use in his care for others. People will only know that God cares for them when they know what it is to be cared for.

Communication: known in its simplest form as 'keeping people in touch'; this kind of personal contact is itself one way of stating the fact that God loves these people as individuals and cares for them personally.

> "God cares for each one as a person beloved
> and precious and unique, not simply as one who
> has a function to perform in God's plan.
> Pastoral visiting represents that loving, caring

relationship. The pastor visits every member of his congregation, not because he is useful for the programme of the parish, or because he is influential or helpful, but simply because he is one of God's children to be loved and respected as he is."

Those words from Dr Newbigin are a reminder that even such a mundane activity as 'keeping people in touch' represents an important statement about their ultimate worth. They are God's children.

Commitment: the ultimate objective in all pastoral caring is "to bring each one into God's presence as a mature individual in union with Christ" *(Colossians 1:28)*.

"Nothing less than this can be the goal of our pastoral ministry. The purpose is that every member of our congregation should be a fully functioning member of the body of Christ, taking his full share of Christ's saving work in the world, fully united with Christ, seeing and judging secular events with the eyes and mind of Christ, fully involved in the life of the world as one who is in the world as the agent of Christ."   Dr Newbigin again!

Not surprisingly, the quality of the pastoral care offered is often found to be a key factor in churches that are growing numerically. It is surely to be expected that where people are befriended and supported, where they are cared for, prayed for and prayed with, and surrounded by a warm-hearted fellowship where love and respect for them abound, hearts will move in response and commitment will grow.

An important pastoral note

The primary purpose of this book is to assist those who have come into the eldership for the first time but, hopefully, it will be of help also to those who have had previous experience of the ministry of the elder. The chapters which follow suggest simple techniques that can be adopted to develop relationships with those for whom we have accepted a caring responsibility.

Three points need to be emphasised if these techniques are to be really helpful.

1. Techniques can help in the development of relationships but can never replace the genuine concern, care, and affection which are at the heart of all good relationships. Techniques are but tools to help us make effective the qualities in a relationship which encourage people and build them up.

2. Some of the techniques suggested are designed to foster perceptive relationships. As relationships develop we must avoid judging people. In a pastoral relationship it is all too easy to become judgemental. Supportive relationships thereafter become almost impossible. Once we are standing in judgement, we are standing at a distance. Judgementalism takes us away from people rather than closer to them.

3. We must safeguard confidences. If we feel the need to share something we have been told in confidence, we should seek permission before doing so. This may mean that sometimes we have to mask a person's identity when requesting prayer support for him or her. It will almost certainly mean that from time to time we will possess disturbing knowledge that has been given to us in confidence.

One of the most frustrating aspects of all pastoral ministry occurs when we know something but have no apparent means of doing anything about it. We must do, then, the most practical thing we can do. We must put the matter in the Lord's hands. We shall continue, of course, to ask for God's blessing on the person involved and give thanks that he will not withhold it.

Thereafter, we need to be ready to take action when he opens the door to new possibilities. However we mustn't feel disappointed if it becomes clear that someone else must take that action. It is sufficient that our prayers have been answered and that God has blessed the one for whom we have been concerned. We must give thanks to the One from whom every blessing flows!

Relating to our people

Elders are given the same basic equipment for developing relationships as anyone else. It is the gift we possess of two eyes and two ears.

Observing

Our eyes will tell us a great deal about the people for whom we are asked to care. Through them we will begin to build up a profile of each individual and each household in our care. Our eyes will tell us much about their life-style. We will learn much just by looking at their homes, both inside and outside. A flush of flowers or the dominance of the kitchen garden; the absence or presence of books and what kind they are; these and many other signs reveal their interests and tastes. People's lives are littered with signs that are clearly visible to us. Through them we build up a picture of what people are like.

But it's important that we don't presume. The real person may be hidden behind what we see. The person who appears very flamboyant may in fact be a very timid person. The solitary person may be someone with a deep yearning for friendship who has been so badly hurt by a let-down in the past that he or she is now very afraid of what could be another painful experience.

It's a useful exercise to check how often we use the phrase 'I presume'. For each time we use it, there will be a far greater number of occasions when it is an unspoken factor. But we need to be cautious even if it's a phrase we seldom use. A wise man once said "Ignorance slays its tens, presumption its thousands."

Listening

We need to use our ears as well. We need to listen carefully to our people -sometimes listening as much to what they don't say as to what they do say. The person whose conversation is always full of the cost of things may be telling us that they are financially hard pressed and could do with some extra help (note the "may be" for in practice that is not always the case) while the pensioner who never mentions financial needs may in fact be too proud to do so. As we listen carefully we shall notice that people speak in different tones at different times. These varied speech tones give us an indication of inner feelings and can often alert us to areas of real need. They tell us too about the spirit that is within a person.

It's important, then, not to become judgemental. We'll never get to know someone completely. Our impression of them will always be provisional, but that's quite enough for us to begin to care for them - to start to pray for them as real individuals and in family groups, and to relate to them in ways which express the interest and friendship of the church. In doing this we strengthen in their lives the affirmation of God's love for them.

Even in its simplest, most basic form, this is a spiritual ministry. It is the fulfilment of Paul's prayer for his people that they might know "the breadth and length and height and depth of Christ's love" *(Ephesians 3:18).*

A wise balance

We have been given two eyes, two ears, and one mouth. The ratio of these basic faculties provides us with a useful guide when we set out to develop our pastoral care.

Once we have been set apart as elders, we experience pressures to get on with the job. We want to show that the congregations's trust has not been misplaced. As we get into our work we shall meet situations where we feel that we must do something. We shall also have the expectations of the congregation as a constant spur. It is all too easy to let these pressures mislead us.

It has been said that we have two eyes, two ears and one mouth for good reason. With one eye we are to see our people, and with one to see what God has done and is doing. With one ear we are to listen for the Holy Spirit speaking, and with one to hear what our people are saying. And only when we have used our eyes and ears carefully are we commissioned to speak.

Meeting the needs of our people

It is easy to feel we know what the needs of people are, and easy in consequence to get them wrong. We need to safeguard against presumption. The blind person may be standing on the pavement looking somewhat helpless, but that does not necessarily mean that he wants to cross the road! We need to discern people's real needs.

In an earlier chapter we noted that the task of the elder is essentially a ministry of encouragement. We are to encourage our people to be what they already are, the people of God. That means encouraging spiritual liveliness, moral improvement and self-effacing witness. All these objectives derive from a particularly Christian understanding of ourselves. They are expressions of the needs that stay with us as we travel through the years of growing Christian discipleship. Stated in this way, however, they could easily suggest a prissiness that would make our relationship with others simply overbearing and quite unacceptable to most. So we need to translate these objectives into heart-warming words and actions within the every day affairs of personal and family life.

If we are seeking to encourage people, to build them up as Christian disciples, and to tell them that they are loved and valued for themselves, we shall need words that carry the message plainly and activities that will embody that message. We shall need to use our eyes and ears carefully. We shall need to identify and meet the practical everyday needs which often enable us to convey the message without actually using the words. There is an important truth in the slogan 'say it with flowers'. So, the offer of a lift to a meeting actually says 'you have a place among us'. The offer of sitting, whether for children or aged relative, says 'we really do value having you with us'.

But we must use our words carefully as we explain what we are doing. The frequently heard explanation 'it was the least I could do!' doesn't actually sound like Good News.

There are two things that we can all do in preparation to meet our people's needs. The first is to do some practical planning. The second is to pray for discernment.

Practical planning

It is quite useful to make a tabulated list of all the people in our care, household by household. Then we make a series of columns related to the needs our people may have. We can make it simple to begin with but allowing sufficient space to keep a note of things which we may find helpful in the future. So the headings on our sheet will look something like this:

Names in Household	Communication	Friendship	Practical Needs		
			Sitting	Transport	Others

Under Names in Household we can jot down such things as the proper spelling of names so that we get them right when writing to people on their birthdays and anniversaries, for example. It can be helpful to have such a memory aid for children living away from home and for other members of the family that we might meet from time to time when they come to stay. There's even value in noting the names of family pets!

Under Communication we put down the ways in which our people hear the invitation to share responsibly in the life of the church. If they come to Sunday service, we put down 'notice sheet', adding a note to remind us if this cannot be relied on because they come infrequently. 'Church Magazine' can also be added and, if they come on to church premises regularly, we could also add 'posters' to indicate that they might see the notice boards and other advertisements. We shall quickly begin to see where the gaps are and to discover the areas we may need to cover.

As we get to know our people we will discover that many already have friends in the congregation. Friendship is an important channel for informal concern and support. People's friends are our allies in providing pastoral care. It can be very helpful to be aware of these friendships. By keeping a note of them we can also get to know where there is a lack of friendship. A lack of friends can indicate a need for us to be more active in linking people into the fellowship of the church.

The importance of friendship

God grants people spiritual gifts to be used. Friendship within the Christian fellowship is vitally important if these gifts are to be identified and developed. Through Christian friendship God does two great things:

◆ He helps individuals to become what he wants them to be;

◆ He releases into the community the gifts of leadership and ministry it requires.

Fostering friendships is an important part of pastoral care. The more friendships people make in their first six months in a church the more likely they are to go on to be leaders in the congregation in the future.

Under <u>Practical Needs</u> we simply note the things that might improve the quality of life for our people. These will be far more diverse than the few categories listed above. They might include help in identifying clearly the stations on the radio of the elderly person whose sight is failing; finding someone who can help with the complex official forms that have to be completed and returned; or simply dog-walking when someone is sick.

Some may have reservations about keeping notes of the kind suggested above. We must clearly understand that any notes we keep are strictly confidential and are kept for the sole purpose of helping us to be better elders through loving our people more effectively. As part of that, our notes will guide and inform our prayers for our people. And that may be the greatest gift we can offer them.

The prayer for discernment

We often speak of 'reading between the lines' of a letter, meaning that we see a reality that isn't actually written down. John Newton speaks in one of his hymns of "the hearing ear" and "the seeing eye", two capacities we bring together in the one word 'discernment'. We need to be discerning in our care for people. Isaiah recognised long ago that such understanding is a gift from God. So we need to pray for discernment; perhaps like this:

> *Gracious God, you know everything I do and understand all my thoughts; grant me your gift of discernment in my caring as an elder, that I may look and listen with true understanding and become the channel of your heart-warming love; in the name of Jesus Christ.*

Prayer

The first element required for successful pastoral work, whether for ministers, elders or others, is prayer. It is not too much to say that prayer is the key that opens the way to all things pastoral.

Praying for our people

Though it is almost certainly teaching grandmother to suck eggs, it needs to be said again and again that without prayer **for** the people in our care we shall not care for them in the distinctive way our faith makes possible. Prayer marks the difference between a club or organization and a Christian fellowship. The church is a fellowship or it is not a church.

Praying is caring

Praying for our people, even if we do not get to see them very often, **is** caring for them. Sometimes we know of needs which are particular to a moment in time - sickness or bereavement, for instance. Sometimes we see needs which belong to the ongoing general circumstances - difficulty in making friendships, struggles over faith and worship, family anxieties, for example. And sometimes we know so little about people that even the general situation offers little guidance.

Our prayers, therefore, will vary in content and from time to time. Some teachers of prayer maintain that it is sufficient simply to bring a person by name (using the Christian name wherever possible) or by face consciously into God's presence.

What is certain is that the Holy Spirit will take such prayerfulness and use it. If we pray for people we don't visit; we shall find we are prompted by the Holy Spirit, that openings are made - and the time is made available even in the busiest life - for us to go and visit them. How this happens is a constant mystery. It is enough to affirm that it does happen and to offer the prayer that makes it possible. Visiting (often wrongly viewed as 'practical caring') grows out of praying. **The prayer is the really practical part.**

Setting out in prayer

When there is a prompting to go visiting we are faced again with our own uncertainties and lack of confidence. So we need to go on praying even as we stand on the doorstep. Some years ago the Revd Kenneth Hibberd suggested a helpful prayer framework for such an occasion:.

Father, I don't know the person on the other side of this door. I've come to be a friend, so will you please prepare us both for friendship. Thank you, Father.

It can, of course, be easily altered to suit the circumstances. But we should not forget what brought us to that doorstep in the first place. If our presence there is a response to the prompting of the Holy Spirit within us, then the way for our visit has been made ready. Even though we feel inadequate, we should go with confidence and good courage.

Encouraging prayer

Quite obviously the fellowship whose leaders pray for those in their care will be the better for it. But even stronger will be the fellowship where the members pray for one another. Paul taught his churches to do good to everyone "and especially to those who belong to our family in the faith". Praying is the highest form of doing good. So we should seek to encourage our people to pray for each other.

Sometimes we know the people and the situation well enough to ask people to pray specifically for someone else. But we must always take care lest this slip into a spurious form of prayer which is nothing more than tittle-tattle in disguise.

However, there are ways we can encourage mutual prayer.

1.   When we come across situations of particular concern, we can ask - in whatever terms are acceptable to those involved - for it to be included in the Sunday service intercessions, or placed on the prayer list if there is one. It can be helpful to have a prayer request book/sheet in the church and for it to be known that the church will be open regularly even if only for a limited time for people to make their own entries. **Prayer requests should only be channelled into the wider fellowship if permission is given and then only in the terms agreed.**

Even though we can't share a particular need with others in some way does not mean that we cannot ourselves pray for the people involved. The simple knowledge that we are praying can be a powerful help to those in need.

2.   Some churches have devised ways of encouraging people to pray for each other as an organized part of the life of the fellowship.

♦   By arranging for a prayer request book/sheet to be available in the church as mentioned above.

♦   By circulating the names on that list to particular people who are pledged to pray for them.

♦   By dividing the whole church family list into various forms of groupings and by asking everyone in the church to pray for some part.

♦   By a system of 'birthday' praying - everyone, just everyone, has a birthday, even if they prefer not to count the years.

♦   By an emergency prayer 'ring-round' designed to cope with those times of dire distress which everyone encounters at sometime or other.

♦   By arranging a specific time for prayer before services or meetings when those who come concerned and anxious can unload their burden in fellowship before other things have to be attempted.

♦   By using our regular diary in a positive way, making a note of one or two people or perhaps a household that we will remember for a few moments sometime during the day. Better for us to do this than to wonder all day about that elusive answer to a clue in the crossword!

The above are not exclusive or exhaustive but simply set out to indicate some of the things possible. Busy people may tend to opt for the informal through fear of yet more organizing to do, so it is helpful to remember that it is sometimes possible for housebound or otherwise inactive people to do such organization. It remains true, though, that informality in this matter can often mean nothing is done.

Most of us will readily admit that in our busy lives things and people are very easily overlooked or forgotten. For many of us some **planning for our praying** may be the only way to keep a check on ourselves and to ensure that **all** our people are supported regularly.

Praying with our people

It is one thing to pray **for** people and quite another to pray **with** people. Though modest in personal claims for the success of any aspect of our ministry, many of us would speak more confidently about our ability to pray for people than we would about our readiness to pray with people. Prayer with people raises all manner of issues.

When to pray? What to pray for? Such questions present an apparent urgency but are of little importance. The really pressing question for most of us is to do with our sense of personal worthiness for this ministry.

Preparing ourselves to pray

There are several basic principles to remember when preparing ourselves to pray with our people.

1.   Not one of us is a minister or elder because we are worthy. We have our ministry because our peers have seen in us spiritual gifts. They have set us apart to use those gifts. For us to decline to use them on the grounds of unworthiness is to dishonour the God who has given them to us, and to be disobedient to the Holy Spirit under whose guidance they were discerned. It is also to demean the trust that our peers affirmed in us when they called us into service. We cannot honour God or our fellow church members unless we use the gifts he has endowed us with.

2.   Our sense of unworthiness is itself a thing of grace. It reminds us that we are utterly dependent on God both for the ministry to which he has appointed us and as we work at it day by day. If we seek to minister because we feel we can do it, we shall certainly fail. Our ministry is possible only because God makes it possible.

      When feelings of unworthiness occupy the heart and mind, they are best pushed a little bit to one side to let in some thankfulness. We need to be grateful to God that he has reminded us **to trust him**.

3.   Our ability to pray is of no great consequence but our willingness to try to do so opens the door to heaven itself. Our most eloquent prayers are but rough-hewn sighs and groans spoken by those whose use of words is always inadequate.

Strength does not lie in the quantity or vitality of our words. Rather it is to be found in the unspeakable grace of the God who hears the incoherent murmurings of his people and understands them. It comes from the enabling work of the Holy Spirit who takes our stammered words and interprets them to our Father in heaven *(Romans 8:26-28)*.

4.   It is generally true that we come more easily to pray **with** people if we are regular in our prayer **for** them.

The practice of praying with people

Some of us may have to pluck up courage when first we come to pray with people and we may feel very vulnerable. It may be helpful to remember that God wants us to pray with confidence. He doesn't want us to be afraid of him - "Let us, then, hold firmly to the faith we profess. For we have a great high priest who has gone into the very presence of God - Jesus, the Son of God. Our high priest is not one who cannot feel sympathy with our weaknesses. On the contrary, we have a high priest who was tempted in every way that we are, but did not sin." *(Hebrews 4:14-15)*. That's a wonderful passage to hold in mind because it speaks about God's desire to receive our prayers for others and also reassures us that we shall ourselves find his grace helping us just when we need it. That gives us a firm basis from which to approach the whole matter of praying with our people.

It may also be helpful to keep some practical matters in mind.

1.   Most commonly, we face the question of whether to pray with people when we are in their own homes; when, that is, we are their guests. We must respect their hospitality. This remains true when we are with people in residential care or in hospital. The fact that we are called to the work of ministry does not give us proprietary rights. We must respect people's integrity.

2.   We need also to beware of giving the impression that prayer is only for serious situations. Many people will appreciate it if we offer to pray with them in times of crisis. Not to do so then may well heighten their distress. But prayer is not a crisis help line. It is an expression of an active relationship with God within which are held our troubles **and** our joys.

So we need to remember the Psalmist's maxim - "It is good to give thanks to the Lord". We shall undoubtedly share with our people times of gladness when we ought to be lifting both them and ourselves up to God in thankfulness.

3.   To be aware of the need to keep a balance, however, does not of itself answer the question "When should we pray with our people?" Sometimes people will make plain their desire for us to pray with them but often they will give no clear indication what they expect.

Perhaps the best way of answering this is to ask them a question. "Would you find it helpful if we pray for a moment before I go?" Sometimes the question can be 'floated' in a personal reflection on the situation. "Maybe we should lift all this up to God and ask his help." Usually such an approach will clarify the position and quite often the reply will be "I'd like that."

Don't be taken aback by a negative response. Once, in a hospital visit, the patient replied "Good God, I'm not *that* ill!" Actually he was but his integrity had still to be respected. So the prayer had to be a silent prayer *for* him rather than a spoken prayer *with* him. He died peacefully the next day.

4.   Even when we have listened carefully to what people are telling us, we may still be unsure what they want. When this situation arises, we can always ask people what they would like us to pray for. A question of this kind can have incidental benefits. It will sometimes enable people to get things into focus and it can show us what other areas of support may be helpful. But more importantly it can prevent us leaving them with a sense of disappointment at the end of our visit.

5.   On the other hand, we may sometimes be quite clear how people would like their prayers answered but find ourselves thinking that God may have difficulty in granting their requests. In such situations we must beware of the temptation to arrogance and presumption, both of which are component parts of judgementalism.

Unless we keep a careful check on ourselves, we may find that 'our' prayer is heard by our people as a rebuke which actually separates us from them. By showing where our sympathy lies, we slip into preaching instead of praying. Something like this is more likely to be of help:

Almighty God,
you have made us wonderfully
   and know all our thoughts;
grant now the illumination we need
that ...... and ...... may know the path
      you want them to take
      and be encouraged to walk along it
      with confidence
      and in company with your Son, Jesus Christ,
for whose promise
      never to leave us or to forsake us
      we give you our thanks.   Amen.

6.   There is a lot to be said for doing some prayer preparation before going visiting. Our people don't have over-great expectations. They're not expecting us to behave as though we had a university degree in the art of praying. They are more likely to be helped if we keep our prayers simple.

There is no reason why the collect form of prayer cannot be prepared as an outline and tucked away in the mind to use, by filling in enough detail to make it personal and particular, as and when appropriate. Perhaps something such as this would serve:

Almighty God,
you have given us the precious gift of life
      and hold us in the arms of your love
      all our days,
bless ...... and ......
that they may have sustaining confidence in you
      and, in the peace you give,
      find strength to cope day by day,
through Jesus Christ our Lord.   Amen.

There is nothing to stop those of us who fear that our memory will let us down at the critical moment from putting the outline on a card to be kept in the pocket or handbag for use when necessary.

Caution!

The moment we feel a loss of liveliness in our prayer or we sense it is becoming the done thing, we must change it to take account of the spiritual growth we have gained but are now at the point of frustrating. It's time for us to launch out in faith once again. Perhaps even time to trust God to help us pray without our card?

Sharing the burden of prayer

Even when we have tried preparing a prayer card we may still find that it is far from easy to pray with people. Knowing the right moment to find out their wishes can be difficult and we may find that even when we feel that this is the proper time to pray together we are still at a loss. At times this may be because we are simply confused, at others because our courage fails us.

When we do experience such times of uncertainty and inadequacy there are two things we can do. Both can prove immensely helpful and can be adopted even when we have actually prayed with our people.

1. We can point to a time when the fellowship will be meeting. It may be on Sunday or at some other time. And we can say . . . 'if you will pray about this for yourself at such and such a time, there will be a larger group within our fellowship who will be praying with you and asking that your own prayer will be all that it is in your heart to say to God'.

    If this idea is adopted, we must not let them down whatever we do!

2. We can identify with them by openly admitting our own difficulty in praying. Admission of our common humanity is the only way to get alongside some people. However, as we want to give them strength and not leave them more isolated than before, we can't leave it there. But we can offer to bring along someone from the fellowship, someone we trust, who will help them to pray.

    We need to remember that this is an exercise in pastoral care, not an evangelical enterprise designed to get at them.

Praying for ourselves while out visiting

Ofttimes when we go visiting one question above all others will be in our minds, "What shall I say?" Jesus knew that this question would be in the mind of his disciples. He gave a specific instruction to them about this when he sent them out 'visiting' *(Matthew 10:12)*. And he followed this with a more general, but no less specific, assurance that they need not fear being lost for words. The Holy Spirit will help them to say what has to be said *(Matthew 10:19-20)*. That same assurance is given to us: the Holy Spirit will guide our conversation.

We must reckon to set out in the power of the Spirit made possible through prayer. The simple arrow prayer offered as we listen to other people speaking - 'Lord, give me the words needed for this moment' - will open the way for the appropriate reply. Instead of thinking on the way home what we should have said, we shall find that thoughts and ideas that surprise us are given at that moment. And later we shall hear the testimony 'you really don't know how helpful your words were'. This may amaze us but it should also encourage us to try the exercise a little more confidently another time.

Preparing prayers

There is no fixed form of prayer that must be used on any occasion. Some elders feel comfortable leading an extempore (unwritten) prayer, but others feel a need to write the prayer in advance. This practice can help to clarify thought, to control length and time, and to give courage when the moment comes to pray. Where elders are asked to share in this ministry it is an important part in the total worship of God's people. It's useful to note down the purpose for praying at that particular time or point in a service before actually trying to prepare a suitable prayer. For instance:

The *Vestry Prayer* paves the way for those exercising ministry within the worship and provides both reminder and reassurance that we minister not in our own strength but in the strength that God gives.

The *Post-Communion Prayer* expresses the congregation's thanksgiving to God for his ministry to us as we have received from our Lord's hands the bread and wine and directs us onwards into the day by day life of the world.

Many variations are possible within these primary focuses. Some elders find it helpful to contact the minister leading the service a few days in advance to find out if there are any special themes or concerns that can helpfully be included in the prayers.

There can be no doubt at all, though, that many new elders find leading prayer the most difficult part of our work. We must say to them, Don't despair! He who has called us will enable us! **The Lord won't let us down.** We can learn how to prepare a prayer, and our confidence can be built up.

Learning to prepare a prayer

Happily we can draw on the treasury of our Christian heritage. The collect, one of the most beautiful traditional forms of English prayer, offers a helpful five-part framework, as the Collect for Purity clearly illustrates.

The Collect for Purity:

The relationship   *Almighty God,*

The faith in which we pray   *to whom all hearts are open, all desires known, and from whom no secrets are hidden;*

The petition   *cleanse the thoughts of our hearts by the inspiration of your Holy Spirit,*

The purpose   *that we may perfectly love you and worthily magnify your holy name;*

The ending   *through Christ our Lord.   Amen.*

Both the prayers in the previous section have been built around this frame-work. Each part of the collect can be extended and there are several traditional forms of the ending. But complexity isn't a requirement of effective prayer. To express the thoughts of one's heart simply and directly is the biblical way of prayer.

It may be helpful to use a layout sheet such as that set out on the next page. Such a guide allows the various things that have to be taken into account to be seen at a glance and enables them to be brought together in an orderly manner that will assist those being led in prayer.

One advantage of working in this way is that it allows adjustments to be made quickly and easily should these be required at the last moment.

Prayer needed for:

Special focus to be included:

The relationship

The faith in which we pray

The petition

The purpose

The ending

$\bigvee$isiting

For many people visiting is a problem. This is so in a general sense. It's not uncommon to hear one partner in a marriage lament that it's impossible to get the other to go anywhere. For some, even the thought of having visitors can bring all manner of tensions to the surface. So it cannot be assumed that all elders will take to visiting as though born to it.

Already it has been noted that there is a widespread misconception about visiting. For many in our churches, visiting constitutes the 'practical' aspect of pastoral care. An elder (or minister) who visits regularly will be counted 'good', one who doesn't will be criticized and may even be made to feel guilty about it. It's important, then, to sort out one's thoughts about visiting and to adopt an approach that can be sustained with peace of mind until changing circumstances require an alteration.

The Statement on Ministry in the United Reformed Church does not mention visiting. It speaks of "pastoral care and oversight". Thus, while the responsibilities that fall to the elders when they take counsel together are specified, the techniques to be adopted when working out the meaning of "oversight" and "pastoral care" are not.

It is a serious error to imagine that there is one pattern of pastoral care that is universally applicable. No two churches have identical circumstances. There is ample opportunity for elders to respond to their own situation in the best way possible to ensure that everyone within the family of their church is properly cared for.

Visiting must be seen in this context if future problems are to be avoided.

The significance of visiting

1.　　Visiting is not a neutral activity. It is focused either for or against the people called upon. In disturbed and troubled times, two questions come quickly to the mind of those being visited: "Is this a peaceful visit? Is this a friendly visit?" Those we call on who are in any way anxious about their relationship with the church will have such questions in mind. People do not automatically assume that our visit is 'for' them.

Even when a visit has to do with a matter of church discipline - which in a corrective sense may not be very often - we need to make it clear that our visit is 'for' and not 'against'.

2.   Visiting in a Christian context has to do with imparting blessing. It was for this purpose that Jesus sent his disciples out with instructions to visit *(Luke 9)*. The disciples were given authority and instruction so that the people of the towns and villages they came to might know that the power of God had visited them. They were to act so that the presence of the God who 'visits and redeems his people' would be made plain. St Paul had a similar motivation in mind when he wrote about his plans to visit Corinth *(2 Corinthians 1:15-2:4)*. The visit (and the letter - a non-physical visit!) is to be interpreted as a working together with the Corinthians for their own happiness. This working together-with is the activity which tells them how much the Apostle loves them all.

3.   Visiting is one of the signs that God will look for in the Final Judgement *(Matthew 25:31-46)*. This sets it in the context of provision for the whole person:

- food and drink	(nourishment)
- hospitality	(acceptance)
- clothing for the naked	(personal dignity)
- care for the sick	(compassion)
- visiting	(community)

It is therefore a matter of great importance. But we mustn't forget that this provision for the whole person is the responsibility of **all** who come under Judgement, not just of the elders.

Going visiting

Visits may be either planned or spontaneous, and planned visits may be either formal or informal. We shall need all three types of visits at one time or another.

Planned visits

Though churches vary enormously, every church has a list of the people who are associated with it, united in membership or linked through a looser affiliation. Every church, whether large or small, is therefore able to plan its approach to visiting. In every church there is a disposition to see that some visiting is done, even if this is delegated to the elders and the minister.

Whether working on a large scale with a multiplicity of elders' groups, or in a small church where formal groups may be inappropriate, it is possible to plan the visiting of those in the church's care. The object must be to ensure that everyone within the community of the church experiences the love and care of the church.

This objective will only be secured if it is planned. If we don't plan the pastoral care of our congregations it is not likely to happen. The logic of planning the overall pastoral care of the congregation is that each elder given a list of people to look after must plan the care within it.

The actual plan adopted may vary considerably from place to place and from elder to elder. But it will probably need to allow for two forms of planned visit. The formal visit and the informal.

The *formal visit* is likely to be one in which we have been asked to find out certain information from the members on our list, or the call is being made in response to a known pastoral situation such as a birth in the family, an accident, or an illness. In such circumstances it will be an act of kindness to telephone in advance to discover a convenient time to call.

In any case, the telephone call to arrange a visit may help us to make the best use of the time we have available.

The *informal visit* is likely to be that made when dropping in the newsletter, the pop-in call to convey birthday wishes, the "casual" over-the-garden-wall conversation which results in an invitation to come in for a cup of coffee, and so on. In village and small community situations the informal visit may be somewhat replaced by a talk while out shopping or in the queue at the Post Office. But we mustn't be misled by the frequency of such contact with some into losing sight of the others in our care.

It is unlikely that we shall develop pastoral care in any depth if we visit only when there is some item of church business or personal concern to be dealt with. There is very good reason to include some socializing in our visiting. The visit 'without strings' can sometimes do more to deepen personal relationships than any number of formal visits which inevitably carry concealed pressure points.

If we are going to keep a balance within our visiting, we shall have to keep some record to check what we are doing. Such record keeping can help us to make calls when we can be reasonably confident that our presence will be appreciated - that is, we will be seen as a sign of blessing. We must keep such records confidential!

Spontaneous visits

If we are praying regularly for our people and we are visiting them also, we will probably find from time to time that a name will come into mind for no apparent reason. This may happen when we are actually on the way to visit someone else, in which case we shouldn't be surprised if our planned visit proves to be shorter than we had allowed for, or if our informal visit finds no one at home.

What probably is happening is that the Holy Spirit is guiding our ministry. We need to respond to the name that came to mind. Call in to see that person. Time and again when such promptings are followed up, the caller is greeted with words such as "Thank goodness you've come. You're just the person I hoped would call!"

Even if we don't get that response at that moment, there's no need to be disappointed. The Holy Spirit may in fact be preparing the ground for what is yet to be.

So our response needs to be one of faith. We need to thank God that his Spirit does prompt us, and then commit that pop-in call to his providential use for the long-term blessing of that person.

Ten rules of visiting

1.   We must always remember that we are visitors and never forget the four cardinal words **"May I come in?"** These words are a courteous beginning to a conversation and will often get us into someone's home. But, to infirm people who can't get to the door themselves, they are words that preserve personal dignity and the offering of the gift of hospitality.

2.   We mustn't outstay our welcome. We must watch both the clock and our host's body language - either or both will tell us when it is time to go. But we do need to stay long enough to have a meaningful conversation with them.

3.   We must be prepared to receive. Any healthy relationship is a two-way process. As a visitor we have gifts to offer to those we visit. We shouldn't be reluctant to accept 'gifts' in return. In particular, when visiting the elderly or infirm it is helpful to accept the offer of a cup of tea, and to let them actually make it - even if it is painful to watch them struggling to do so.

4.   If we say we'll do something, we must do it. If we find we can't do it at once for some reason, we should provide an update.

5.   We must guard with our life anything told to us in confidence. If help seems to be indicated, we should seek permission to ask the minister to call.

6.   We mustn't encourage closet critics. If a cause for concern arises, particularly a criticism of some kind, it is unhelpful to offer to pass it on or to take it up anonymously. That way stunts growth. It is far better to help them present their own case, even if we don't agree with it ourselves.

7.   We should avoid firing other people's bullets. We must never, just never, use someone else's concern or complaint as an excuse for firing off a few matters of our own. We must have the courage to accept full responsibility for what we want to say. Mention others only with their permission. People won't trust us if they feel we will misuse what they say to us.

8.   It is wrong to apologize for taking up someone's time. Their time and ours alike are given by God to be used in a way that honours him. If we need to apologize for wasting their time, we're wasting ours.

9.   A phone call or a postcard can be as valuable as a visit but cannot be a perpetual substitute for one.

10.   The counter balance to the visit is the invitation. Our personal circumstances may not always permit it, and we shouldn't feel badly about it if they don't, but where they do the invitation to group members to visit us at home can be a sign to them that a genuine relationship is being sought.

Giving and receiving

In a living relationship there is an interflow of activity between the participants. This can be characterised in several different ways but one of the most useful is that of **giving** and **receiving**.

The gifts we offer

Time: Pastoral care takes time. It takes time to develop a relationship. It takes time to do whatever may be required within a relationship. It takes time to support and sustain a relationship.

For most of us called to the eldership, time is a premium commodity. Its use needs to be planned on the basis of sustainable priorities. This is why we have given some consideration elsewhere to ordering our priorities.

Skills: While there is much to commend in the saying

"Don't walk in front of me, I may not follow;
Don't walk behind me, I may not lead;
Just walk beside me and be my friend."

there is more to pastoral care than simply friendship.

We are called to pastoral care and leadership because the congregation has discerned certain gifts and abilities in us. These need to be drawn out and trained if our full potential is to be developed. The gift and ability mix in the individual elder varies enormously yet, whatever the combination, it is a significant feature within our giving to our people.

We must not, however, think that we are simply to try to use 'spiritual' gifts in our work as an elder. If we are developing a real relationship with our people we will be concerned also for the everyday things of life. A truly spiritual understanding of our people will see the *physical* need as well as the *spiritual*. It could well be that the most caring thing we can do for someone would be to provide a bag of firewood in the middle of a cold winter or, in this all electric age, a fuse for that spare heater that hasn't worked for some time.

Though we may feel inadequate in a particular situation, what we are able to offer will almost certainly be sufficient at the moment.

Ourselves: Some pastoral visitors use phrases which actually speak of a lack of giving: "I had a few minutes to spare so I thought I'd pop in". Kindly meant, no doubt, but well capable of conveying the message "I haven't really got time for you!"

Others are tarnished by their very professionalism. "I shan't be in on Thursday; that's my day off." Everyone knows we have to have time for recreation and renewal but such statements may well convey a different message. "Our relationship is strictly professional." While this is entirely acceptable and indeed the only way of handling many areas of human need, it won't do in a truly pastoral relationship.

The lady had been in acute distress for many years. She had been referred to all manner of consultants, and tried a variety of counsellors. One evening her life was transformed. When asked what had happened, she told how a man unknown to her had come and conversed with her for an hour or so. "Others", she said, "had given me their time and their skills. He gave me himself."

The pastoral relationship, in some sense, is to *embody* the God "who neither slumbers nor sleeps" *(Psalm 121:4)*, the God who gives himself to his people.

The gifts we receive

Trust: Even the act of being invited into a person's home is a sign of some degree of trust. The more a relationship develops the more trust should grow. "I'd trust her with my life!" - not always a statement based on mature judgement but always a declaration of a person's belief about the direction in which a good relationship should be developing.

We must take care, then, not to abuse that trust.

Burdens: The old lady said to the young minister "You can't put an old head on young shoulders; I shan't tell you any of my troubles". But as time went on she found she could trust her minister. She began to open up her heart and to off-load some of the many burdens she was carrying. Burden sharing is the mark of a developing relationship. A problem shared is a problem halved. The simple act of being willing to accept someone else's confidence can make all the difference to them.

It can also make a world of difference for us if we accept their burden as a weight to be carried. "So many people come to me with their problems", said one carer, "that I don't think I can take any more". For this reason, all of us should have a support structure of some kind. If we feel the pressures mounting, we need to have the good sense to ask for help!

Kindness: The overwhelming majority of the people we have to do with will want to be kind to us. This will show itself in a hospitable welcome, in genuine concern for our well-being, and perhaps the actual presentation of gifts.

We need to respond to the hospitable welcome by accepting it. It's unhelpful to hover on the doorstep saying "I'd rather not come in, thanks all the same". Nor is it helpful to launch into a protracted conversation on the doorstep or, for that matter, in the garden where neighbours might overhear. And we shouldn't feel we have to take a gift in acknowledgement if we are invited round for a meal.

We need to be open to those in our care. Of course, we shouldn't bare our soul in anguish every time we visit. But we do need to give enough of ourselves to satisfy their genuine concern for our well-being. There's nothing worse than someone about whom we have to say "I never felt I got to know him as a person".

"I wonder if you could do with" is often the lead into the offering of a gift in kind. At the height of the produce season, for instance, it's so easy to kill that kindness by observing that "Our own plants are absolutely loaded this year. We just don't know what to do with all the stuff!!" Far better to try to find some way that doesn't stifle the instinct to give. We need to encourage kindness, not nip it in the bud!

As we get to know our people and also the wider congregation we may be able to redirect kindness that we find overwhelming. We can, for example, introduce the idea of giving to other people in the congregation, the more so if we can suggest individuals who would be blessed by a gift. We can offer to deliver the gift or we might be able to use it as a chance to foster the growth of pastoral concern and care by encouraging the giver to take it in person. We should always be on the look out for the opportunity to 'grow' the next generation of pastoral workers and elders.

It will be helpful also to try to channel the kindness of some of our people into the most creative form that it can take. Prayer is a very practical form of caring and it will be well to ask a few of those whom we know to have a kindly and generous spirit to commit themselves to pray for us personally in our ministry as an elder. This will itself open up further opportunities for giving and receiving within the relationship.

Pastoral groups

It's a strange thing that we have so much trouble in the church over pastoral groups! Almost no one is without practical experience of a group. Even if we have never been part of a small group in a church, we have experienced a small group in our family life and will no doubt have been a member of many more groups of one kind or another through the years. So why do we find it so difficult both to lead and to share in small groups in the church?

Perhaps because there is nothing magical about them, groups can be helpful or destructive. There are many groups we become part of because we have no choice. Whether we like it or not, we are part of those groups unless we make a conscious effort to opt out. Church groups, however, are different. We have to make a conscious effort to opt in. Voluntary groups can fail simply because people don't come. This can be because not enough care has been taken at the invitation stage, or because the group does not succeed in holding their allegiance. And even when care is taken over the manner of invitation, previous negative experiences of groups can make some people extremely wary of ever getting involved.

However, all is not gloom and doom. Many, many people are finding small groups a renewing experience and testify gladly to their worth in the life of the local church. Indeed, for generation after generation, the small group has been the way in which the church has kept the faith. It has been the channel through which the individual has been built up in faith, hope and love, and the means by which those without Christ have been drawn into the life of the Christian community and led to the point of commitment to Christ. The small group has been used, and is being used, powerfully by God.

Set out below are some practical matters which may be of help when forming and leading an elder's group.

The reason for groups

The introduction above has given a little of the philosophy behind groups in the life of the church. However a group needs to have a purpose and the leader needs to have that purpose clearly in mind. In the early days of setting up a caring structure, a group may be formed simply to enable people living in a geographical area to get to know one another. Its emphasis may be primarily social. However, it may well gain a different purpose at other times. Once relationships have been established, a group may decide to do some Bible study together, or to work as a group in some project being undertaken by the whole church. It may become a most important care agency as the members pray for one another and also seek to give each other practical support.

Getting a group together

People need an impetus to come together in a voluntary group. Even well-established groups need to be summoned if meetings are to happen. The basic methods for getting a group together are quite ordinary. They're no different in fact from the normal everyday means of communication. Contact has to be established and this will involve one or more of the following:

> The letter or postcard

> The telephone

> The personal call

These may be used better in combination, such as the letter followed up by the telephone call, or the telephone call followed by a visit. It is likely to take time!

Notification or invitation?

There is a sharp distinction that we must bear in mind. A notification of a meeting is not necessarily the same thing as an invitation to that meeting. All too often we confuse these two things. People may need notification that a meeting is being held but they will probably respond better if they receive an invitation.

The welcome

If the preparation for the meeting has been done thoroughly, the leader will have a pretty good idea who will be attending. It is most valuable to know the names of the people expected and to have taken the trouble to find out if possible which face fits which name! But it will be a wise thing in the early meetings of a group to remember that some people really do have a problem recalling people's names. The use of the sticky label name badge can help people to feel at ease in each other's company.

When introducing people, be careful not to give details about them which will come better when relationships have developed a bit. And be particularly careful when introducing anyone new who may have come to the group seeking support in a time of need. Revealing that need to the group during an introduction can be a devastating experience for the person involved and may well prove embarrassing to the group.

As part of the welcome give some thought to where people will sit. Have extra chairs ready. It can be quite embarrassing, especially for late comers, and disruptive for the meeting if the host has to root around in the attic looking for enough seating. Such activity may raise questions about acceptance. "I'm sorry to be such a nuisance" can mean "I'm not sure if I'm really wanted here".

If people don't feel comfortable physically in the group's meeting place, they may well not feel comfortable in the group's company. So have a thought for such things as summer's brilliant sunlight or winter's draughts, and for places to put coats, and so on. If people say they will have to leave early, try to find seating for them where they can do this with a minimum of disturbance to the other members of the group, or to the activity for the meeting.

Leadership

There is good reason for us to share the leadership of a group. All too often people make the mistake - and group members actually encourage it! - of leaving everything to the leader. The consequence of this is that several different functions of 'leadership' are left in the hands of one person in a way that can seldom be handled satisfactorily.

Group leadership requires four things:

> Preparation
> Hospitality
> Leadership of the meeting
> Pastoral/personal discernment.

The development of an effective team to cover these four requirements has several advantages. The first is that responsibility for the success of the group is spread. It doesn't all hinge around one person. Secondly, it prevents any one person becoming so bogged down that the meeting becomes a burden. Thirdly, it recognizes that not one of us has all the gifts that a successful group will need to draw upon. Fourthly, it sets at least one person free to look perceptively at how the group is working, to listen to the silences, and to observe the body language. Such a person can also come to the aid of the leader should emotions become aroused.

We need to keep the purpose of the group always in mind, even when the tasks of leading the group and providing hospitality for it have been passed to group members. When this is done it will be necessary to have a preparation meeting so that the other members of the leadership team know what is expected and can plan accordingly.

Refreshments

Refreshments can come at the beginning, in the middle or at the end of a meeting. Each position has arguments for and against it. At the beginning, refreshments can offer kindly cover to late-comers but can also mean that the purpose of the meeting is pushed late with the hazard that it may not be completed at a reasonable hour. In the middle, refreshments can give a welcome break and a chance for a time of informality but they can also break up the proceedings unhelpfully. At the end, some may want to get away but may feel cheated through missing the informal fellowship; others may simply take root with the resultant frustration for the host who might really like to get cleared up and to bed.

Perhaps the key to positioning the refreshments is to set them firmly within the main purpose of the meeting and within our knowledge of the needs of the people who will be present. If people are coming straight from work, then without doubt some refreshment should be available for them at the beginning. If the main purpose is to get something done against a clear deadline, then the need to deal with the business in hand will probably take precedence.

Ending a meeting

We need to give as much care to the process of ending the meeting as we have given to getting it underway. How will it end? All too often the answer is in confusion and uncertainty. But it does not have to be so.

The leader will need to gather what has been agreed or, after a Bible study or devotional meeting, to collect in a simple prayer the various strands of thought and concern that have been expressed. This should not be used as a last desperate attempt to ram home any doctrine or issue which may not yet have rooted in the hearts and minds of group members! Rather it should be a moment of recollection which expresses confidence in God for the future. The collect form of prayer lends itself to this.

Lord Jesus Christ,
in whose name we have met
and whose presence has blessed our fellowship;
take the words we have spoken,
and our quest for faith, hope and love,
into the purposes of your love for us
and for all people
that we may hasten the day
when everyone shall live in the power of the Holy Spirit
and every knee shall bow and every tongue confess
that you are Lord and Saviour;
to the glory of our God and Father. Amen.

The leader will also need to make sure that everyone knows who should be doing what and ascertaining whether any of them will need help in doing it. It is valuable to get the group itself to provide these extra resources, and time must be allowed at the end of the meeting for these matters to be dealt with.

The date of the next meeting needs to be fixed, together with the venue. For group members the meeting is over when they go home. For leaders there is a golden rule:

⌐ Absent members

The meeting is not over for us until we have informed absent members of the date of the next meeting.

This needs to be done as a matter of courtesy but there is a deeper reason. Members present have had the chance to determine the future of the group which actually belongs also to the absent members. Often it isn't practical to reconsider a date once it has been fixed but absent members should be given maximum opportunity to adopt that future for themselves. All too often the die-hard attenders become a clique whose date-fixing ability excludes others.

It is a good thing, therefore, for the leader to have some idea when the group should meet again. Those who send apologies can be asked before the meeting about two or three possible dates so that the leader is able to include them in when arranging the future date.

The place and rôle of devotions

There is much discussion in the churches about the place and role of devotions in a group meeting. There is no doubt that for some people they form 'the religious bit' and many group members will assume that devotions are 'the done thing'. On the other hand, many group leaders find the devotions the most difficult part of the meeting. Many feel uneasy about reliance on the various books of opening devotions which are available. So it may be helpful to give some thought to what the devotions in a meeting are all about.

Our group is meeting as an aspect of our life together in the Church. Within this setting there are several points we need to consider.

♦   We meet because we are part of the people of God. So it is helpful to have that affirmed.

♦   We are caught up in the loving purposes of God for ourselves and for his world. It is helpful to be reminded of that.

♦   We have a task of some sort at the heart of our meeting. It is valuable to open ourselves to the gifts and graces in others, and to the guidance of the Holy Spirit, before setting about that task.

♦   We need to be lifted out of our complacency. Goodness doesn't just happen! It has to be thirsted for by those who want to see God's Kingdom come. It is good to have our appetite whetted.

♦   We are fallible people and our meetings are not proof against the destructive forces which groups can sometimes release. Our meetings need to be safe-guarded by the love of God.

In that setting, there is an overwhelming case for undergirding a meeting with prayer. Very often this will best be expressed by having opening devotions. However, nothing is more likely to crab a cheese and wine party! Discretion is needed if we are to give sensible leadership. This may mean that the leaders will meet to pray together for a short time before everyone else arrives. Many find such a practice helpful anyway but doing this before a social evening, in which a normal pattern of devotions may feel quite awkward, does mean that the key leaders are themselves prepared as fully as possible.

Setting up group meetings

It is difficult to offer a Readers Digest style DIY Guide to setting up a group meeting in a manner guaranteed to work. This is because of the many different situations in which our ministry is exercised. What is appropriate to one will be quite unhelpful somewhere else. However, the following points should prove of some help in evolving a strategy for group meetings. Before using them, there are two things that require some thought - the nature of the group and our own strengths and weaknesses.

The nature of the group

The notes we have kept from our individual contact with the members will prove of value in getting an overall view of the group. What kind of people are they? What's their wavelength? Are there any common interests among them? Where do we sense they are spiritually? Who are their friends in the church? What concerns do we know they are carrying? Have they a spouse who does not share their commitment within the church but whom they must always consider? Are there children involved?

The overview provided by the answers to such questions will help us to deal with the major question: who is it that we want to meet together?

The expected answer might be 'everyone' but this is not necessarily the best answer. If, for instance, we have a sense that numbers could be so great as to make a full meeting unsatisfactory, it may be better to seek smaller meetings with the aim of blending them from time to time to enable people to meet one another on a wider basis.

Such consideration of the group can also point to the most practical time for meetings. Sunday afternoon might be a better time than Tuesday evening for a group composed mainly of commuters who do not get home before 7.30 p.m., for instance. A group that has within it several farming families might find it difficult to meet during harvest time, while one covering a number of elderly single folk might be better served by a morning or early afternoon meeting rather than one in an evening. And, of course, if we want a meeting or event at which we want the children present, we shall have to fix a time suitable for the children to be out and about.

Our strengths and weaknesses

We must be aware of our own strengths and weaknesses, **Particularly our weaknesses**. Not all of us are cut out to be group leaders! The gifts we have may be of a different kind. Dr George Carey, appointed Archbishop of Canterbury to lead the Anglican Church through the 90's, recalls a period in his life as a parish priest when he was in personal difficulty. He shared his feelings with a friend. "I find myself in the puzzling situation of working from my weaknesses rather than my strengths." He was rather disconcerted to receive the reply, "Praise God for teaching you the importance of working from the weak areas of your ministry. The majority of clergy refuse to allow God to teach them this and then stop growing." Having thought about it for a while Dr Carey commented: "Working from the weakness in my ministry might be just the very thing that God wanted for me . . . if through this I could enable others to grow."

There is a serious point here. So often we feel that our weaknesses prevent us from taking effective action. They certainly mean that we shall not work either effectively or happily if we constantly seek to do the things for which we have no gift or aptitude. But weaknesses need not prevent us from caring effectively for our group, so long as we are honest about them and put them in their true setting.

Our weaknesses did not prevent God from calling us into his service as elders. By acknowledging them honestly we shall grow spiritually and begin to share the experience of the apostle Paul. He wrote "When I am weak, then am I strong". This was his reflection on our Lord's answer to his fervent prayers to be set free from his 'thorn in the flesh'. "My grace is all you need, for my power is greatest when you are weak" *(2 Corinthians 12:9)*.

By admitting our weaknesses, and developing ways of working through them, we shall help more people to grow than in any other way. This suggests that we should try to involve others in sharing responsibility with us for the life and health of our group. A general resolve to involve others in our care and leadership - and the group meeting is a good practical area where this can happen - will also help to ensure that the church has capable leaders in the next generation.

Evolving a strategy for group meetings

In developing a strategy for group meetings several questions need to be considered carefully:

1. **What is the primary aim of the proposed meeting?**

   ♦ for fellowship get-together
   ♦ for friendly get-together
   ♦ for sharing of church business or concerns
   ♦ for Bible study/prayer meeting
   ♦ to consider topical local or national issue
   ♦ other

2. **Who should meet?**

   ♦ the whole group
   ♦ only some of the group   - those with a common interest
                                             - those from a geographical area
   ♦ including children and non-church spouses
   ♦ including others   - from within congregation
                                     - from beyond congregation
   (N.B. If only part of the group is to meet, for whatever reason
   Keep the whole group informed to avoid misunderstandings.)

3. **Where should we meet?**

   ♦ in the home of the elder
   ♦ in someone else's home   - within the group
                                     - elsewhere within the congregation
   ♦ somewhere else   - at the church
                                     - in the open air (picnic, outing, etc)

4. **How often should we meet?**

   ♦ as frequently as the group decides
   ♦ on a regular basis
   ♦ when special need requires

5. **Who should organize?**

- the elder
- the elder plus invited helpers
- helpers on behalf of the elder

6. **What should organization cover?**

Once you have decided who will organise the meetings, the following matters require careful attention.

- Invitations, including guidance to location

- Hospitality arrangements, including briefing of hosts to cover numbers attending, refreshments, car parking, and clearing up after meeting

- Agreement on apportionment of responsibility between the elder and any helpers, and also the elder and meeting leader where the elder is not actually to lead, including

  welcome and introductions
  opening devotions
  introducing the topic
  leading the discussion
  agreeing any follow-up
  setting date for next meeting (and topic)
  thanks to hosts
  closing devotions

- Notification as a **matter of urgency** to those not present of the date of the next meeting

- Thanks and encouragement to any helpers, including review of success of arrangements, noting any improvements needed next time.

Our ministry to children

"It isn't easy going to see the Smith's," she said. "The children never go to bed and it's difficult to get a conversation without them being there." "I know just what you mean", replied another elder, "but I find another problem even more difficult. How do I relate to the children? It just isn't possible to call to see the children without seeing the parents also. I don't feel that I can visit them without asking the permission of their parents and I feel most uncomfortable about asking to talk with them without their parents. It looks as though we are trying to hide something!" "I wish our church had that kind of problem," added a third, "Trouble is we are such an aged congregation that we haven't had children about the place for some years now."

That snippet of conversation highlights the confusion felt by many of us when we come to consider the children of the families in our care. Most of us instinctively relate far more readily to adults than to children. The presence of children actually poses a problem for us. It raises the question, "How do we as elders work out the appropriate pastoral care for the children in the households we have been asked to look after?" That question personalises the wider issue of the way in which, as a congregation, we look after children.

It is important to emphasise at once that we have responsibilities because of the requirements of the Children Act 1989. The Act is designed to foster good practice in the care of children and should be welcomed. It relates particularly, though not exclusively, to our corporate responsibilities and has a special regard for the care of the under 8 year olds. Various pamphlets are available which describe the effects of the Act. These should be taken into account by all churches reviewing their work among children or planning new developments.

These issues of corporate and individual responsibility are closely knit together but it will be helpful to deal with them separately as two aspects of the one question "What is the proper responsibility of the elder for the children of the church?"

Our responsibility as an Elders' Meeting

Elders have a central responsibility for the children of the church. *The Basis of Union* says that elders are responsible together "for the institution and oversight of work among children and young people" *(Section 2:2(2))*. In other words, the elders have a key rôle in ensuring that the children of the church are properly cared for. Our rôle is to superintend. Where, however, there is no formal provision for the children in the church, we have an initiating rôle. It is our task to ensure that provision is made for the needs of the children.

Oversight

The exact way in which this will work out in practice will vary from church to church according to circumstances. In churches which have a Junior Church or Sunday School, the rôle of the elders is to ensure that the leaders are given every help and encouragement. It is our responsibility to ensure that the care given to the children is the very best.

This may mean instructing the Finance Committee or Church Treasurer to include more allowance for children's work in the annual budget and stimulating the church members to find the money needed. Or it may mean encouraging **and** enabling the leaders to attend training sessions. It will cover such matters as preparation for baptism and may mean reminding those who see the children as 'the church of tomorrow' that they are properly part of the church of today, with their own levels of faith which must surely be as acceptable to God as the faith we have as adults.

In churches where regular leadership for the Junior Church is often very difficult, it may mean securing the support of the church members for patterns of all-age worship that allow the children to share with the adults instead of being separated from them. In some churches it may mean finding supplementary help for the leaders. In too many churches the task of securing any assistance in the Junior Church or other youth organizations is left to the leaders themselves, even to the extent of finding their own successors when for good reason they have to give up the work they have been doing.

It is all too common to hear good people, including Sunday School teachers and youth leaders, saying "I felt so guilty about giving up. I felt I was letting them down". Many of us know leaders who didn't give up when they should have done. Part of our leadership as elders should be to ensure that such matters are handled with sensitivity. It cannot be in the best interests of our children for them to be cared for by people whose heart is not in it or who are riddled with guilt at even the thought of retiring. Equally it is part of our responsibility as elders to have the courage to 'release' leaders who really should no longer be teaching. To let matters drift on for fear of hurting or upsetting people is to deny our children the proper care we are charged to provide for them. It is in matters such as these that we set the tone and temper of the church's care of its children.

Initiative

It is all too easy for us to become complacent about the work our church is doing among children. For the most part we have left behind the days when the health of the Sunday School was judged by the amount in its Post Office account. But the reckoning that was behind that kind of assessment is still with us. Numbers count for a lot. If our Junior Church numbers haven't dropped, all must be well! If they happen to have increased, then all must be very well! Perhaps it is, but it is easy to be blinded by numbers. Undue attention to numbers may mean that we are not asking about the quality of the teaching the children are receiving. We need to be asking about their growth towards Christian maturity and whether we are really doing all that we can to encourage that.

We need to be keeping an overview. What kind of care is actually being provided for the children by their leaders? Are they visited when ill? Are their birthdays remembered? Does anyone trouble to find out why they haven't been for the past three weeks? Other questions are equally important. Is it time to be training up new leaders so that others can be released from work they have been doing without a break for many years? Do we in fact know such personal details of these stalwart servants of the church? Is there work that needs to be done amongst the parents so that they can support the care and teaching given by the Junior Church?

In such concerns we need to be working in close cooperation with the leaders themselves. Some readers may have winced at the suggestion in the previous section that we should 'release' those who should no longer be teaching. The thought of it is enough to cause panic in some Elders' Meetings. Perhaps panic is justified if the only time we pay attention to what is happening in the Junior Church is when there is a crisis. If, however, we have a relationship with the leaders that is characterised by ongoing encouragement and support, the atmosphere should be right for us to initiate changes.

Imagination

The number of children within the congregation is used by some as a measure of the ability of the local church to survive. "There's no future for this church," said one senior elder. "You see, there are no children any more." When that sense is around, the absence of children has become a problem, sapping the ability of the leaders of the congregation to give effective ministry to the people who are there. The absence of children has become a dispiriting element in the life of the church. There are two things that can be done about this.

Challenge the assumption: Is it really true that a church without children has no future? The answer may well depend on the kind of community we are in. In an overwhelmingly retirement area, there may indeed be few children but that may not prevent the church being a growing church. There may be more than enough retired folk to regenerate the congregation and also to enable it to grow. But even if the community itself is declining, and there are indeed no children about, the challenge is to care for the community that does exist. We should not allow such a ministry to be denigrated simply because once there were children and now there are none.

Ask the question: "Is it inevitable that this church has no children within it?" To answer this we must search out the facts. Are there children in the local community? All too often elders will say that theirs is a retirement area without children when a cursory glance at the supermarkets will make it clear that this is nonsense. There are children in the community. The challenge, therefore, is to make contact with the children who are there.

However many there are, it is likely that only a very few will be linked with any church. We need to ask "Why don't these children come to our church?" What stops them? Are our programmes wrong? Are our times of meeting too awkward to fit in with patterns of family life today? Does our image exclude rather than welcome? Is our provision too narrow? Are there specific needs to be met? Could we provide for children who are handicapped or disabled? Could we do something to support and encourage one parent families? Only when we have faced squarely questions such as these shall we be able to take the appropriate steps.

Do the research: How can we find out why our church doesn't have any children? Some of the information we need will be of a general kind but some will be specific to our own church. Generally speaking, people working in the community, such as school teachers (particularly those in the first and middle schools) or governors, health visitors, and pre-school play group leaders, will be very happy to share with us their understanding of the situation. There may even be a school or youth organization working with the Duke of Edinburgh's Award or similar schemes which would be happy to have some of its entrants conduct a survey to find the answers for us.

Harness the goodwill: A wise Congregational layman used to emphasise the goodwill towards the local church which exists in most communities. He often lamented that this valuable resource went largely untapped. This is because the predominant thinking in many congregations is of the church as a provider for its community, not as a receiver of what the community can do for it. "We have a Gospel of Good News for you but you have very little, if anything, for us", seems to be a fairly common attitude. But one of the important things the community does have is contact with many people that we don't meet.

One way forward for the church without children is to harness the goodwill of the community as a first step. Many share with us deep concern for the children in our communities. What is there to prevent us inviting some of those who share this concern, such as the folk mentioned above, to meet with us informally to discuss what can be done? And to do this without the presumption that it can only be done safely if we do it ourselves or have total control over how it is done. An initiative of this sort would need our involvement as elders, and our leadership to carry it through.

Use imagination: We need to use a lot of imagination in our Elders' Meetings. We need to dream dreams and then to let the creative spark fly as we share together in addressing the problem. Too often, we lack imagination. Too often, we're afraid to create precedents. Too often, problems met in the past are more dominant than the vision we have of the future. Too often our answers to recurring problems are but a recycling of the past, so much so that in one church the minute books have identical entries written by different church secretaries twenty years apart! Yet it is our privilege as elders to be amongst the first to trust the promise of God, "Behold, I make all things new" *(Revelation 21:5)*. Nowhere should this be more evident than in the way we take seriously our responsibility "for the institution and oversight of work among children and young people".

Watchful attitudes

Sadly, much of our children's work is marked by self-interest. Parents will volunteer to assist in the crèche or with the Junior Church so long as they have children in them. All too often their enthusiasm wanes sharply when the children have moved on a stage in their development. We can advance a number of reasons to explain this but seldom stop to think about the overall image we are presenting to our children.

Clearly we must not respond to this by suggesting that parents should neglect their children. Nor must we simply take note of a prevalent attitude in society in a spirit, if not of condemnation then certainly of lament, that we have so much difficulty raising up leaders for work among children and young people. Rather, we must find practical ways of asserting the things we do believe in.

Parents' self-centredness starts when their children are at an early age. It's at this age that the baby-sitting circle offers them a chance of an evening out. It would be wrong to suggest that they don't need these times of recreation. They certainly do. However, recreation means, if it means anything, replenishing the gifts we have received so that they may be the more fully used in the future. If people are to use and develop the gifts they have received, they must be given opportunities to exercise them. It is all too easy to encourage them to put their gifts on 'hold' by adopting a 'when the children are a little older' attitude. This is not good for them as parents and certainly not good for their children.

Can we secure baby-sitters to enable people to use their gifts in service to others? Can we offer transport to get their children to the various activities that seem to dominate so many families today, thereby setting parents free to serve others? Can we work with them to release their gifts for the benefit of the community? And can we take more seriously than we do the need to ensure that the crèche staffing rota is not made up mainly of parents? The crèche is supposed to set parents free to worship.

These are but some of the attitudes about which we need to be watchful. But there are others of a different kind which have a bearing on the way we respond to them. Do we assume that we have to meet the needs from within the church community? Elders in small churches may have read this far and already concluded that these ideas are alright for larger churches but they are beyond their own small congregation. Elders of larger churches will know that such problems are not limited to smaller churches. It seems that all churches have recruitment problems. We need to ask whether the answers to these questions can be found in the goodwill towards our church in the surrounding community?'

In this respect the Children Act offers a helpful pointer. It requires close cooperation between the various statutory and local authority bodies that have an interest in the care of children. We need to ask some questions far more often than we do. Who can we share with? Who can we invite to cooperate with us? That is, we don't have to do it all ourselves for it to be done well.

Community awareness

Without doubt, there is goodwill towards the local church in most communities. But how much real goodwill is there in the local church towards the community it is part of? Are we praying that the local school will find the parent governors it needs? Are we undergirding the scouts and guides with our prayers? Do we ever respond to the public invitations to come along to the mother and toddler group tabletop sale? Do we go along when the local school has its fête? Are we prepared to campaign for the council to provide an area where young people can skateboard in safety and with a minimum of nuisance to others? The list is endless once we begin to develop a community awareness.

We often hear people say 'do as you would be done by'. It is a good biblical principle. If, then, we want people to come along when we advertise events, we should be alert to events going on in the community and support them. Indeed, if we support only the children and youth activities of our own church, we are as much guilty of self-interest as anyone else. And we teach others by such things. Clearly we can't do all these things ourselves. What we can do is to ensure that such matters are included in the conversation when our church talks about work among the young. We can try to ensure that encouragement is given to the church community to be broad in its interests and warm-hearted in its response.

In such ways we can show that our care for the children and young people of the church is a fulsome one. We shall fail to do this if we show interest only in what is being promoted by our own or other churches. On the one hand, we shall falsely separate sacred and secular and, on the other, we shall reveal a spiritual arrogance which, whether we mean to or not, denigrates those who provide for children and young people in other ways.

Caring for the children on our pastoral lists

There is no doubt that the problem outlined in the introduction to this chapter is a real one. Most of us do find it much easier to relate to adults than to children. There are a number of reasons for this.

The problem of access: How can we visit the children without the parents being present? The honest answer has to be, 'only with the utmost difficulty'. Indeed, there are some who would advise that we should not seek to see them apart from their parents. Good reasons can be advanced for such advice. There is the ever present fear of putting ourselves at risk, perhaps through children mistaking our intentions. There is the danger of creating mistrust or misunderstanding between the parents and the children. And there is the possibility of damaging the relationship we have with the parents. We may think that there are minimal grounds for such fears and, taking each in isolation, we may be right. Taken together, however, the risks are considerable.

The problem of relationship: What relationship are we seeking with the children. It can scarcely be the same as the one we have with their parents. In our relationship with them there is something beside friendship. There is at least an implicit recognition that we have been set apart by the church to a ministry relating to this household. Older children may begin to have some idea what this means but usually a relationship with the children will be predominantly one of friendship. Even this may not be easy to develop. Children's friendships ebb and flow, and are shaped by peer group pressures, passing interests and shared activities. In many instances, these seem increasingly to separate the children from the adults as adolescence approaches. So even where a good friendship is established it may prove very difficult to sustain a lively contact as the years pass.

The problem of definition: What do we mean by the 'pastoral care' of children. The corporate responsibility of the Elders' Meeting has already been explored. But how does this relate to the individual elder face to face with the child of the household? What is the elder supposed to do? How far should matters be pressed if, for instance, a child says that he is worried by something? Even with our own children it is easy to give a wrong answer or to supply more information than our children are seeking at that moment. With a sick adult we may feel it right to ask if it would be helpful if we prayed together before bringing the visit to an end. Can we do this safely with a child? Should we even consider it without the parents being aware and on hand? Are we the best people to do it anyway or would it be done better by someone with whom the child has a more direct relationship?

There is a further area of concern of which we might become aware. We need to be very sensitive and very careful if we have any feeling that any form of abuse may be underlying a child's anxiety. Abuse needs to be dealt with by those who have the training to do so. We must keep such feelings to ourselves, sharing them only with our minister. We may never know if there is real abuse, but if our feelings subsequently are confirmed, our prime task is to undergird the **whole** family in prayer and to be ready to give such practical assistance as the family may in time be open to receive.

These are but some of the many concerns that may arise in our pastoral care of children. They indicate the complexity of the matter. Taking all the areas of difficulty, it may appear that there is very limited scope for us to develop pastoral care for the children on our lists. That impression is surely wrong, except in so far as it suggests that our pastoral care of children will be in some sense different from the care we offer to the adults. There are at least two positive elements that we can identify as appropriate in our care of children.

Inclusive activities

One way that elders with a specific care list which includes families with children can adopt is the inclusive activity. All too often our meetings are mainly for adults. Very often they are arranged in the evening and for purposes which are ill-suited to the inclusion of children. This becomes all the more apparent when our hosts children won't go to sleep and are brought down 'to sit quietly'. It usually isn't long before some toys are produced but quickly rejected for a slithering game behind the settee, much to the group's distraction and the embarrassment of the hosts. In this situation, the children are present but not included.

However, given the different setting of a group family barbecue or picnic, and the children will feel included from the beginning, even more so if there are games for all ages to play together. The fact that adults can have fun as part of their life in the church is an important lesson for children to learn. Church need not be dull and boring! Similar benefits can come from church family away weekends and the like.

In whatever way, the important thing is that children are included in ways that don't separate. We are familiar with the term 'the community of women and men' which has arisen from the attempts being made to break down the walls which for so long have separated male and female within the church. It is just as important that we develop the life of the church as 'the community of children and adults'.

Not all of us feel comfortable with children. So perhaps it will be helpful to remember once again that it is alright for us to involve others in the leadership of our group and its activities. Inclusive activities need to be led by someone who can inspire both children and adults. Securing that is just as much part of the pastoral care we are charged to provide as is talking with the youngsters themselves. And perhaps the point at which our duty becomes our delight.

Creative prayer

The point emphasised in the chapter on prayer, that prayer is the most practical activity within our pastoral care, needs to be further emphasised in our care of children. There is no finer gift we can impart to them than our prayers. There is nothing more likely to undergird an ongoing relationship with them than our prayers for them.

There is indeed nothing better that we can do to secure God's blessing for them. God has a purpose for each of them. Each one needs help in discovering that purpose and 'owning' it for themselves. The way has to be prepared if that is to happen. Before they can do it for themselves, windows of opportunity need to be opened for the Holy Spirit to move as he will. This is, in part, the task of Christian parenthood; in part, it is the task of the Christian community as it cares for the young. Our role as elders, especially in the larger congregations, can be crucial if that part is to be effective.

One minister recalls how during his teenage years, when church-going had become something to be avoided, two people in the church in which he grew up never stopped praying for him. From time to time they found ways of reminding him of what they were doing. It irked him more than a little. Some years later he was called to the ministry. Looking back, he was convinced, he said, that the prayers of those two people during his difficult adolescent years were a vital part of the preparation for the call to ministry to be heard and answered positively.

The various methods outlined in the earlier chapters for making our care systematic and our prayers regular and informed, can all be used effectively to assist us in praying for children and young people. And these can be reinforced if we also positively affirm their special days - their birthdays and other days which mark the stages in growing-up, their personal achievements, and so on.

If, in our prayers, we have positive attitudes towards the children and young people as individuals we shall be the better placed when matters of policy or discipline have to be tackled.

Our ministry to sick people

The visit that we shall need to make most commonly is the sick call. Indeed, we may find that this is our first introduction to some of those within our care. The sick visit is not only something about which most of us feel an inner compulsion and sense of priority, it is also the occasion, perhaps more than any other, when people may feel neglected if we do not visit them.

It is well worth spending some time considering our ministry to the sick and the following topics will open up some of the concerns we need to address:

- personal feelings
- people's expectations
- the setting of our ministry
- ministry as an expression of the grace of God

Personal feelings

Our own attitude to sickness and suffering will have been shaped to some extent by the attitudes of our parents or of those closest to us when we were children, and it may also have been influenced by our own experiences of sickness and suffering when we were very young. Those early influences will have been supplemented by more recent encounters with sickness and suffering. These may have confirmed our childhood feelings but they may just as well have resulted in us now having radically different thoughts and feelings on the subject. Furthermore, our thoughts today may be affected by teaching we have received or by books we have read.

In practice, many of us are more than a little confused and not at all consistent when it comes to the matter of sickness and suffering. We experience confusion personally when we are ill. In many stages of life, we will reject illness and fight strongly to live; later on, perhaps, we may view illness as the prelude to entering eternal life, or at least as a way of escaping from mounting inner frustration, as infirmity more and more limits our quality of life and makes us increasingly dependent on others. It is likely that these varied feelings will be with us when we are visiting the sick and will shape our conversation or at least affect its tone.

Other people, too, will have mixed thoughts and feelings on the subject. Broadly speaking, we are likely to meet two main attitudes to sickness and suffering. We shall meet rooted opposition to the very concept of illness, opposition undergirded both by the mores of contemporary society which invests so much energy and funding in health promotion and care, and by a strong Biblical sense that sickness and suffering do not belong in the Kingdom of God. Those who hold this view will rightly point out that some four-fifths of the recorded activity of Jesus is to do with healing the sick.

We shall also meet people who acquiesce in the face of sickness and suffering. While they may not deny that the immense public health programme is right for the nation, they may ask whether the individual has an inherent right to permanent good health. They may express doubts about the wisdom of the organ transplant programme and the over-strenuous efforts that doctors are sometimes thought to make to keep elderly people alive. Those who hold such views may point out that the Bible appears to show that God can use sickness within the purposes of his love, that Jesus did not heal everyone he came across who was sick, and that there are very many people who are severely afflicted and suffer constant pain, yet are radiant and Christ-like.

There is not the space within this book to unravel the theology of sickness and suffering. It is enough for us to recognise that we shall meet great variations of thought and feeling as we go about our ministry. We shall find these variations within ourselves and it is more than likely that as we gain experience in visiting the sick we shall find that our own thoughts and feelings change.

It is particularly important that we don't allow our feelings to react negatively with things we may find deeply shocking. If we do we shall most certainly become judgemental and the opportunity for creative ministry will pass. We need to remember that there is usually a reason why people say or do the things they do. For instance, we may find it deeply shocking that a man never visited his wife while she was in hospital having their first child. Her explanation that he couldn't stand the smell of hospitals seems very lame. Yet the husband may have this phobia because he is recalling unknowingly the hospital visits he made as a youngster when his mother or father or grandparent was dying.

Or again, the woman who has no time for illness and appears to have little sympathy with anyone who is sick, especially those who are nearest and dearest, may have watched someone deeply loved enduring a painful death. Her family's illnesses reawaken the hateful power of that experience. They raise doubts about her ability to cope. They speak about dying and death, and she's very frightened of both. So much so that she will be angry when members of her family are ill.

It's easy enough to feel shocked when someone is cross because her child is ill. Set in the context of the parent's life, that anger is actually a measure of the ministry needed. It is important therefore to try to minister in a way that does not limit the potential for the grace of God to meet people whatever their thoughts and feelings about sickness and suffering or whatever our personal understanding.

People's expectations

For the most part people will expect us to be what we are, fellow church members with a particular concern for them. They will expect us to be elders, not mini-ministers or healers, but they will hope that we shall, in some sense, exercise a ministry towards them.

This ministry has several parts to it. These include

- ◆ affirmation of their personal worth
- ◆ representation of the church's concern for them
- ◆ undergirding at a time of personal need
- ◆ opportunity to feel 'in touch' with God
- ◆ reassurance of support for their family
- ◆ sympathy and understanding that go deeper than words.

Each of these parts could be explored in some detail but it is sufficient for our present purpose simply to identify them. There is no formula to be applied when visiting the sick. There is no right way to do this or say that, though there are some ways that may be more helpful than others. Essentially the sick visit springs out of the relationship between people and will be as varied as the people involved.

There are, however, some things to remember. The first is that our visit is an aspect of the overall ministry of encouragement to which we are called. That doesn't mean we must be optimistic in every situation. Our good sense will tell us when we need to be realistic and not to get involved in creating wrong expectations. We shall, however, want to make the visit such that the sick person, and the ones caring day by day, will feel in some sense we have improved the situation.

Sometimes we get an insight into this when people greet us with the words "she always seems better after you've been" or "he does so much look forward to your visits". It's very difficult to define just what it is about a visit that leads to such results. Perhaps it is just a matter of relationships, but more likely it is to do with the grace of God. If we prepare ourselves in prayer before we set out and if we visit in a prayerful manner, it is reasonable to expect that the visit will have a special quality that will make it enriching no matter how sick the person is.

Secondly, we need to keep the conversation and overall approach as simple and straightforward as possible. The guidance to ministers - KISS - found in a Guernsey pulpit is a memorable acronym for use in the sick room. It was actually a weekly message from the minister's wife to her husband - "Keep it simple, silly".

The old man had been visited by the local minister through all the stages of his illness. Their conversations had moved from downstairs to upstairs, and then back down again as the sitting room became a temporary bedroom. One day, when the old man was bedbound, he asked the minister if he could say the prayer at the end of their talk. The minister was happy to go along with this and was deeply moved when the old man prayed:

> *Gentle Jesus, meek and mild,*
> *look upon a little child;*
> *pity my simplicity;*
> *suffer me to come to thee.*

That prayer, learned in early childhood, summed up everything the old man wanted to say and just over an hour later he died.

The lady was well into her 90's and very poorly. She hadn't spoken much all day and the bedside communion service was kept very simple, a tiny fragment of bread dipped in the wine. Just beforehand the 23rd Psalm was read in the Authorized Version that she had learned in childhood. Immediately the reading began she spoke it word for word, calling forth the riches of God's grace stored long years in the treasurehouse of her memory. Words spoken with conviction. Simple words, releasing an inner strength.

So it is for many people. The older they get and the closer to the decisive hour, the more it is the simple words and ideas that express best their thoughts and feelings. The more that we can discover what those are for any particular person and reflect them in our ministry at the bedside, the greater will be the blessing bestowed on them.

The context of our ministry

What has been written in other chapters about the shared responsibility of the Elders' Meeting needs to be remembered when we come to our ministry to the sick. We are in a very personal relationship with the sick person but we are not alone. Our own ministry is an expression of the care we seek to give as a corporate responsibility of the Elders' Meeting. It is therefore a matter of regret that such aspects of our ministry as care for the sick do not receive the same degree of thoughtful consideration within our meetings as do many more mundane concerns.

How fulsome is our concern for the sick? In many congregations it is possible for people to be ill without many knowing about it. While it is true that some people prefer not to be the focus of attention, it is more true that this is precisely the moment when the reality of Christian fellowship is most under scrutiny and so often is found to be lacking. When this happens the result may be that the elder or minister is accused of indifference or poor visiting, or the church gains a reputation for not caring.

Such an outcome is a clear sign that the context of the minister and elder has been lost. We need to remember that we are part of the church community. Any community that is going to function effectively needs structures to help it do so. The rôle of the minister and elder has sometimes been emphasised so much that the importance of the congregation's own rôle in ministry has been neglected. Within the understanding of the Reformed tradition, ministry is the task of the whole people of God. Because we recognize that some do have special gifts, we set apart some people to be carers in the congregation. But we must beware lest that encourages everyone else to abdicate their proper responsibility to care for each other.

Hence we need to have well organized structures to allow the special caring gifts to be used most effectively, while also emphasizing the personal responsibility of every member to be a caring person. This balance needs to be redressed in many churches. There are two things we can begin to do as individual elders that will help to get the balance right.

1.   As we get to know the people on our care lists we shall find that they have different gifts. We should watch out for those who have a strong interest in people and a lively faith. These are the folk we should ask specifically to undergird our own ministry with their daily prayers. Missionaries often affirm that it is the knowledge of the prayers of others that makes their work possible, specially in the more difficult times. We too will do our work better if we are aware of a constant undergirding and strengthening through the prayers of others.

2.   We can share the responsibility for the care of the sick with the people on our care lists. Most of us will want to do a fair amount of the visiting ourselves but there is good reason for us not to do it all. We shall help people to grow if we encourage them to share the work with us. We need to apply the creative dynamics outlined in "Giving and receiving" on page 51, while clearly understanding that we must be sensitive to the needs of the sick person as we do so.

Our ministry to the sick begins long before anyone is ill. It begins as we plan together in Elders' Meeting to ensure that our structures are effective. We need to address such questions as:

- ♦ Can we be sure that we become aware very quickly if anyone is ill?
- ♦ Does that awareness extend throughout the congregation or is it limited to those who are prominent in the fellowship?
- ♦ Is our ministry coordinated so that minister and elder do not call on the same day?
- ♦ Is our ministry sustained throughout a person's illness, or is it enthusiastic at the beginning and patchy as time goes on?
- ♦ Is the focus of our attention on the sick person or does it include the needs of the whole family?
- ♦ Is our ministry limited to spiritual matters or does it include day by day practical needs?
- ♦ Conversely, if the emphasis is on practical needs, what must we do to meet the spiritual needs?
- ♦ Does our teaching encourage church members to be responsible for one another, or have we delegated care to specific people?
- ♦ How do we engage the prayer support of the whole congregation when someone is ill?
- ♦ Should we have a special time of prayer for the sick, perhaps as a midweek service or prayer meeting?
- ♦ Are we able to respond positively if any of our members should ask for the laying of on hands or for anointing?
- ♦ Should we appoint some elders to administer the communion to the sick and the housebound, remembering that this requires the approval of the District Council?
- ♦ Is the distribution of flowers after the services an effective expression of our ministry to the sick?

What we do individually as elders needs to be seen in the context of the whole church's care for the sick. It needs the framework of a considered policy of the Elders' Meeting and we should enlist the active support of some of those on our care list.

A gracious ministry

Our ministry to the sick is to be an expression of the grace of God. We need therefore to set about it with as much graciousness as we can. This means that we shall seek to observe the courtesies of life, some of which are set out on page 49 as the ten rules of visiting.

Sick people often feel that they have lost control over their own lives. They are now in the hands of others. It is important therefore to accord them dignity and the chance to have some influence over things. The direct question beginning "May I ... " and the enquiry that starts "I wonder if... " both avoid presumption. By using them we affirm a person's worth just at a time when complete dependence on others may be as much of a problem as the illness itself.

Affirming a person's worth is important at every stage of life. It remains so even when people appear to be grievously ill. It is highly presumptuous to talk about them within their hearing. One family sat at the bedside of an elderly relative in a very deep coma. He was not expected to live more than a few hours. As they talked they divided his goods and chattels between them. A few days later the man came out of the coma with precise knowledge of the items to which each member of the family had laid claim. When he was out and about again one of his earliest calls was to his solicitor to make a will leaving all his estate to charity!

The man was deeply hurt that his estate was more important to his family than he was himself. He felt that the family's greed had prevented them giving him the support he needed at a critical time of his life. He felt that they had diminished him as a person. It was the total loss of worth, the being counted dead before he was, that hurt him the most. His story offers us a vivid illustration of a very important truth within our ministry to the sick. It is important that we affirm the positive things of life even when people appear to be close to death.

Anointing with oil

We must aim at being positive too when our ministry to the sick produces the unexpected. It's very easy at that moment to be anything but positive and to appear less than gracious. One situation that is more likely to occur now than for many years past is the request for the elders to come together to pray over the person who is sick and to anoint with oil in accordance with the teaching in chapter 5 of the Letter of James.

It is very likely that many of us will never have been asked to do this. In fact, the whole thing may be a complete mystery to us. We may have heard the term anointing but have no mental image to give us a picture of it. Or we may have an impression that it is something more to do with the cults than with our kind of church.

One outcome of the renewal movement in the churches is that people are taking the Bible with new seriousness. Indeed there are churches that are developing patterns of healing ministry within which passages such as James 5 are proving influential. The person who asks for anointing may have been influenced by this development and may feel that it is a very proper part of the Christian's response to sickness, an expression of deep personal commitment to God.

We need to be aware, however, that the request may have sprung from an entirely different motivation. If the person who asks is feeling utterly desperate in the face of illness, it is possible that the request falls into the 'when all else has failed' category. It may then have little to do with commitment but rather more reveal the emotions of someone who feels hurt and increasingly let down by God.

How should we react if we are asked either to arrange such a ministry or to share in an anointing? We may find that our first reaction is one of shock. The request goes beyond our experience. Indeed, it may awaken fears since it relates to an area of Christian experience which many associate with signs and wonders. Or it may produce anxiety about doing anything that creates false expectations for the sick person.

The passage in the Letter of James actually says that a number of things are involved. The initiative lies with the sick person to summon the elders. The elders are to pray for the sick person and perform the anointing. Full healing relates to the total person and must deal with the inner realities as well as the physical symptoms. Confession unlocks the door to the inner person and allows the forgiving grace of God to cleanse the depths of personality, the heartland of being.

Easy enough to read in the Bible, not too hard to grasp in concept, but difficult to handle when a request for this ministry meets us unprepared. Indeed we may find it personally very challenging because James also says "the prayer made in faith will heal the sick person . . . the prayer of a good person has a powerful effect" *(James 5:15,16).*

We may feel that whoever this passage is speaking about it cannot be about us. We would not reckon our faith to be the kind that heals sick people, or that we possess the sort of goodness that can have such a powerful effect. So our response to the request for anointing may include having to deal with inner turmoil that is almost as challenging to us as the illness is to the sick person.

The person making the request will probably be quite unaware of the turmoil the request has created for us. Nor, most likely, will there be an awareness of the pressure such a request creates within the eldership itself. On the one hand, there may be the problem of the lack of a precedent - we may want to respond positively but have little knowledge of how to deal with the situation. On the other, we may feel very negative towards the request but recognize that the disappointment of saying no may inflict a lot of hurt. We may feel that, in any case, this is not be the time to start a theological argument about the interpretation of James 5. Within both responses, there will be a proper reluctance to raise false expectations.

Several books listed under "Books" on page 101 deal more fully with the matter of anointing. They reflect a variety of opinions. Some authors regard anointing as a normal part of the church's ministry, while others feel it should be used sparingly. Once, however, we understand more of the background to it we shall be able to prepare a more adequate response should we be asked for anointing. Whether we feel able to support or to refuse we shall find almost certainly that the fearfulness begins to go and that we are released to deal with the situation calmly and supportively for the person who is sick. Our response will also take into account the motivation under-lying the request.

If we decide to proceed with anointing the degree of formality to be adopted will depend somewhat on the seriousness of the illness and the wishes of the person involved. A formal order of service might be used for someone preparing to go into hospital for surgery, for instance, who could be invited to receive anointing in the church or in their own home; indeed it may be well to offer a choice. But for someone who is grievously ill, a very simple informal procedure may be more suitable.

In every case, it must be stressed that anointing has to do with living, not dying. There are many whose memory of anointing will recall it being used mostly in the Roman Catholic Church to prepare for dying. This is no longer the Roman Catholic understanding. Anointing is now referred to as the sacrament of life. This faithfully represents the spirit of the Letter of James.

A possible order of service is included as an appendix on page 97 to assist any elders and churches unable to obtain the books on the Church's ministry of healing suggested for further reading.

A ministry offered in faith

One of the recurring themes throughout this book is the need to remember the setting for our work as elders. We are part of a team. We do not have to tackle things by ourselves, even though we may find ourselves in the position of having to give the first response. Should that situation arise, whether or not we have a prepared response ready for it, we need to ask leave to talk to our minister as a matter of urgency or, if that is not possible, to consult our fellow elders.

The person who makes the request for anointing is asking for ministry. We may not feel very comfortable with what is being asked for, but even a negative response must be offered in the spirit of ministry. We may feel that, for what seem to us to be very good reasons, we cannot agree to an anointing. That refusal needs to be presented with the utmost care. Or we may feel that this is not the time for heaping disappointment upon disappointment and therefore agree to an anointing but with some diffidence.

We must surround either response with equal prayer. When prayerfully arrived at, both responses are acts of faith. If we do proceed to an anointing, we may be confident that our Lord will not reject our stumbling act of faith nor refuse his blessing on the person seeking ministry. If we feel we have to say no, we must be as confident that our Lord will honour that decision also and guide us into deeper ministry which will satisfy the person's need.

Cared for when in deep waters

Fear not, He is with thee, O be not dismayed;
For He is thy God, and will still give thee aid:
He'll strengthen thee, help thee, and cause thee to stand,
Upheld by His righteous, omnipotent hand.

When through the deep waters He calls thee to go,
The rivers of grief shall not thee overflow;
For He will be with thee in trouble to bless,
And sanctify to thee thy deepest distress.

Richard Keen

When people won't respond

A few months into our ministry as an elder, we will begin to realize that people respond to us in different ways. For some we will be a most welcome visitor and we'll have a sense of developing friendship. From others, however, there may be no welcome forthcoming. We will feel a sense of distance and may begin to wonder if our calls are doing more harm than good.

Such rejection can arouse a variety of feelings in us. It may make us anxious about calling at any home for the first time. It may be hurtful and bring back memories of other more painful incidents in our lives. It may leave us feeling guilty that in some sense we are letting the church down. It will probably take some of the shine off our ministry and may make us wonder if we were right to let ourselves be nominated for election. And we may begin to ask the question "How am I going to cope if this goes on?" All of us need a reference framework for our ministry when such feelings occur.

We are not alone

There is not a minister in the land who is the perfect pastor for everyone in the congregation. Not one of us is God's answer for everyone. As is commonly said, "we can't please all the people all the time".

There is, of course, a spiritual background to all this. If we were able to achieve universal acceptance, we would be unlike our Lord! Not everyone welcomed Jesus. This fact needs to be included in our understanding of his words to the disciples "No slave is greater than his master, and no messenger is greater than the one who sent him. Now that you know this truth, how happy you will be if you put it into practice" *(John 13:16-17)*.

Appointed and given authority

Our gifts have been recognised by the church which has called us to share in its ministry. The church has given us authority to do the work of an elder and has promised to support and encourage us.

The church has not said, and will never say to us, "Go and see how popular you can be. Measure your ministry by that." Which is not to say that as a church we must be insensitive to the difficulties an elder is having.

Dealing with them is part of the necessary periodic review of our pastoral structures.

Caring for those who won't let us in

It is unhelpful to focus Christian pastoral care mainly on visiting. Indeed, there may be a number of things that have to happen in some situations before visiting becomes a practical reality. These prepare the way and are among the spiritual gifts which we bring to our ministry.

The prayer of thanksgiving

The people in our care have been given to us by God. That seems to be a sweeping statement but is the only way in which to make sense of our ministry. The pastoral structures we have adopted as a church were not chosen at random. They were carefully thought out and prayed through. They were established as we met together in the Spirit, which was also the setting for our own election and ordination. In a very real way, God has given us to our people and given them to us.

So, above all else, there is the need to be thankful for them. It is quite immaterial whether or not our personal relationship with them appears to have gelled. Even if we feel the pain of rejection, we must still give thanks for them; if they have done nothing else, they have given us a lively insight into what our Lord went through for us.

We must be thankful for the people in our care, thanking God for each one of them individually and irrespective of our feelings.

The prayer of blessing

Although rejection can be very painful, we don't ordinarily associate what happens in our pastoral work with the hate-filled rejection of persecution. Yet it can be helpful to look at that dimension in the teaching of the New Testament.

Jesus says: "Pray for those who persecute you" *(Matthew 6:44)* and Paul expands this when he says "Ask God to bless those who persecute you - yes, ask him to bless, not to curse" *(Romans 12:14)*.

If that was the teaching of Jesus who faced persecution, and of Paul who had done his share of the persecuting, how much more should we heed it when faced with the lesser rejection we shall meet. To pray for blessing on those who reject us is to be obedient to our calling. Our prayer for their blessing will begin to make all the difference.

The prayer of concern

We need to remember that if our encounter with people leaves us feeling ill at ease it is unlikely to have left them with a tranquil spirit. In their own way they will reflect what we are feeling and will probably be confused. As part of our pastoral care for them we can ask the Holy Spirit to use those feelings to create new possibilities.

Part of a team

We will undoubtedly have times when we feel the strains of our ministry. Stress needs to be kept creative and this is unlikely to happen if we keep it all to ourselves. Because stress so often arises from an individual situation, it is usually better if we don't share it with members of our group. Better to share it with another elder, or with our minister.

In some situations, however, this may be difficult. Occasions can occur in which we feel particular pressures precisely because we are part of a team. Often these will centre around clashes of personality or issues of policy. It is sometimes difficult to know whether there is real cause for concern or if we are ourselves a major part of the problem. When this occurs, there can be value in consulting **in confidence** someone outside the situation. This could be an elder in a neighbouring church or the minister of another church, not necessarily of our own denomination.

Wider consultation can also be of immense support when we see a need but cannot see the means to satisfy it. No church has the full treasury of the Kingdom of God located within its own congregation and resources. Yet the riches of the Kingdom are accessible. The key to releasing them is partnership. On the one hand, we need to be far more willing than we often are to share what we have been given. And on the other, we should feel far more free than often we do about asking others to share with us what they have been given.

The benefit of being part of a team is that we can help one another.

When people cease to meet

A potentially painful situation occurs when people in our care cease to meet. Our response will be coloured by the personal relationship we have with them but it may well be determined by a number of other factors, such as:

- the *intentions* of the people involved, in so far as they know them - have they simply ceased to meet, or are they in the process of leaving the church?

- our *understanding* of our church and Christian discipleship - do we reckon our church should be able to provide for all the spiritual needs of the members, or do we think of discipleship having tides and seasons within which some people will move from church to church to fulfil their potential?

- the actual *rôles* people have had in the active life of the congregation.

Against this complex background it is difficult to set out any approach that will be all encompassing but we do need to have some framework within which to work. This framework will differ from church to church, not least because of the differences arising from the varied understandings among us of the nature of the local church and of Christian discipleship. But there are some elements which should be included in any approach we take.

Avoid presumption

The dangers of presumption have already been stressed. It is all too easy to assume that we know why people do the things they do. We need to hear as clearly as possible from the people themselves their real reasons for ceasing to meet. Only when we know what is really going on in their hearts and minds will we be in any position to respond carefully.

Take the matter seriously

It is a curious fact that all too often we give less attention to the needs of those who cease to meet than we give to those coping with other difficult situations. We have groups to support people in marriage crisis, with disabilities, in financial difficulties, and in bereavement and we put a lot of time, effort, and finance to helping them as individuals. We have very few resources earmarked for the help of those passing through times of spiritual crisis.

All too often people who cease to meet are regarded as a problem for which the best approach is 'least said soonest mended'. This attitude is sometimes heightened where there have been previous unresolved tensions. The assertion "It will be better for everyone if they go!" needs careful consideration before we let it determine the way forward.

Allow time

Many people will not share with us the depth of their feelings during a cursory visit. We need time, if they'll give it to us, to establish that our visit is essentially because we are **for** them. What has been said earlier about the purposes of visiting applies here. Only when that has been clearly established by us, and accepted by them, are we likely to have a conversation that will take matters forward. We need, therefore, to allow for two or three meetings with them.

Take action early

All too often we hear people reflecting on their links with the church in the past and they let slip that "no one ever came to ask us what the trouble was". Their inference is that the fellowship to which they had given their allegiance and a portion of their lives did not care for them. "No one ever seemed to care what happened to us."

Now in fairness it has to be remembered that while such things are said sincerely they do not always represent what actually happened at the time. Sadly, however, we are often getting the truth, at least in so far as people had some expectations about how a caring church should respond when people begin to fall away. Whatever happened, their expectations were not met.

The key in all this is to take action early. One reason for suggesting that it is good to have a profile of our members is that it can help us to spot changes in attendance patterns, and to act at once. The sooner we ask people questions which speak of our concern for them the better, especially if we go out of our way to do so. Leaving it until we bump into them in the supermarket will not convey the same message, even if the same words are used.

Release the pressures

The process of ceasing to meet contains a number of inevitable pressures for the people involved. Clearly there are pressures on us as elders, but we need to consider the pressures that the other people may well be feeling. If, as we would hope, our own relationship with them has been amicable, we shall want to talk with them ourselves, assuming that their relationship with us has also been alright. But we need to recognize that most people are very reluctant to hurt others. If there is anything about us personally that is involved in their ceasing to meet, they may be acutely embarrassed if we confront them. This can, in fact, make their problem worse. It can lead them into evasion which will leave them feeling guilty, even more guilty than they may feel already.

Similar forces can come into play where the church really feels that such matters are best left to the minister or church secretary to deal with. People sometimes cease to meet because they have problems with the way in which the church is being led. For them, then, to be visited in the first instance by the very leaders with whom they are already dissatisfied can be totally counter-productive. And it will almost certainly make it even more difficult for the minister to minister effectively to them.

There is here a possible rôle for non-serving elders who are not identified with the present leadership and who may be counted on to listen without a need to defend the leadership's position. Indeed, it could be helpful to appoint two non-serving elders to get alongside those ceasing to meet; they would be impartial visitors who have no personal axes to grind, no need to apologize for their actions, but who have been given the specific task of listening carefully and then taking whatever action is needed in response to what they have heard.

Clearly the size of our congregation will have some bearing on this. It will be much more difficult for small congregations to diversify their care but larger churches could well find advantage in doing so. Even in small congregations it may be possible to have someone other than the church officers to explore the issues that must be resolved if the way is to be opened for people either to join actively once again in the life of the fellowship or to be released without guilt.

Don't cause guilt

Even when people have good reasons for leaving a church (or for dropping responsibilities) they can still end up feeling guilty. Indeed, they may be angry because the fellowship has made them feel guilty. "I don't know where we are going to find someone to replace you" is sometimes used to express appreciation for what someone has done. Unfortunately it is equally capable of being heard another way. "You really are letting us down, you know." It requires a very toughened conscience not to feel guilty.

When people need to be released we must make an effort to set them free as graciously as possible. This seems much more difficult to accomplish in a small congregation but, in fact, the ability of people to induce guilt is probably just as great within the larger congregation because the actual number of people directly involved may be no greater than in a small church.

Whether we are members of a large or small church, we must try to avoid making people feel guilty.

Caring for the non-active member

Only when we know why people are ceasing to meet shall we be able to decide how to care for them.

Where people have made the decision to leave our church they will sometimes know where they are going. If they have made a link already with another fellowship, they may not need a commendation from us. But it may be a courteous thing to ask them if they would like one, even if they are leaving following a dispute. If they haven't made a link with another church, the offer of help to find one, can be one way of enabling them to go in peace. This can, in fact, make all the difference to the ease with which they will settle in another church. Unresolved conflicts are a poor foundation for new relationships.

Sometimes, however, people will simply stop meeting but with no intention at that time of leaving the church. If our church has a strict discipline in these matters tied, for instance, to attendance at communion, we may have no option but to remove their names from the membership roll. However, where we are not tied in this way, it may be better to seek out the real reasons for their decision and to relate our response to these. In this way, we may hope for a constructive relationship which will keep the door open for them to become active again in the future.

Maintaining contact

Whose responsibility is it to maintain contact? This raises an issue which often becomes a source of irritation. It is commonly assumed that it is the responsibility of those who wish to 'keep their link with the church'. The matter not infrequently comes into discussion when such things as printing costs are under review. But is it really their responsibility?

If we have accepted that there are legitimate reasons for us to support their position, the responsibility for providing the care that is needed to maintain their link with the church is ours not theirs. We shall need to resist the pressures that are felt every time someone says "It's no use inviting them. They'll never come!"

If they are not invited

♦ they do not know of the opportunity to come;

♦ they do not know if they'll be welcome if they do come; and

♦ how will they know they have not been completely forgotten?

It is important that we take the initiative. Now, of course, frequently repeated invitations can create an unhelpful pressure and leave people wondering if we really understand what they have said to us. On the other hand, a complete lack of invitation carries its own negative message. "They really don't care about me." One way of dealing with this is to agree a basis of continuing contact as one expression of our care for them.

It is very important that we sustain any arrangement we make. The care we seek to give people is to reflect the way Jesus loves us. We rejoice that he is a man of the utmost honour who does not break his promise. The way we deal with people tells them a lot about us. It should also tell them a lot about Jesus.

When things go wrong

In the life and service of every elder and minister things will go wrong and we shall make mistakes, sometimes grievous ones. Not one of us will be able to sit passively when the prayer of confession invites us to say:

> *Almighty God, our heavenly Father,*
> *we have sinned against you and against others,*
> **in thought and word and deed,**
> **through negligence, through weakness,**
> **through our own deliberate fault.**

We shall know beyond any shadow of doubt that for every occasion on which this is true and known to others, there are tens that are known to us but hidden from sight. We shall join in the words because it is a fair statement of our life and ministry.

Sometimes we shall feel very down-hearted and both unworthy and inept for the ministry the church has committed to us. At such times our thoughts and feelings may lead us towards resignation. They can be very compelling and we need to know how to respond to them.

Clearly this is a subject that could be considered at length. But maybe there are some guidelines that can be of assistance.

1. We must face the fact that we're not perfect. We won't always do the right thing, even when we want to. The apostle Paul knew the problem well. He wrote "the good that I would I do not: but the evil which I would not, that I do" *(Romans 7:19 AV).*

2. We must acknowledge that repentance not resignation is the course God wants us to follow. We need to let the prayer of confession become a statement of our intention to get back on the right path and with renewed resources.

    > *We are truly sorry and repent of all our sins.*
    > *For the sake of your Son Jesus Christ, who died for us,*
    > *forgive us all that is past;*
    > *and grant that we may serve you in newness of life;*
    > *to the glory of your name.*

3.   In the normal course of our ministry we shall know when we have got it wrong and freely admit our responsibility. We shall be only too pleased that we are given the chance to repent, being profoundly glad that our God rejoices when we come to our senses and seek his forgiveness. And even when we find repentance difficult we shall know also that this is a sign of a deep spiritual battle within us. It is one form of Paul's "the good that I would I do not ...". It is sufficient at that time for us to acknowledge this and to seek God's help in getting that good released in us and through us.

4.   We need to confess 'without excuses'. Excuses, even when they are completely true, in some sense off-load our personal responsibilities on to other people. This is a dangerous practice to establish. There are at least three reasons why excuses are to be avoided.

◆   People will spot what we are doing and begin to wonder what the actual truth of the matter is. They may even wonder why we are trying a cover up.

◆   We may well find that when it comes to taking responsibility for ourselves and for our actions, 'acknowledging the sin that is in us', we shall begin to make excuses to God also. Our confession of sin will be diminished.

◆   Excuses, by implication, suggest we do not trust God to forgive us.

We need to trust God by accepting his word to us at face value.

> If we confess our sins to God,
> he will keep his promise and do what is right;
> he will forgive our sins
> and purify us from all wrong-doing.
>
> *(1 John 1:9)*

In summary

┌─ **When things go wrong** ────────────────────────────┐

  Confess to God;

  Apologize, without excuses, to our members;

  Commit the situation to God's grace;

  Get on with the job.

└──┘

Order of service for anointing

Prayer

Almighty God,
to whom all hearts are open,
all desires known,
and from whom no secrets are hidden;
cleanse the thoughts of our hearts
by the inspiration of your Holy Spirit,
that we may perfectly love you,
and worthily magnify your holy name;
through Christ our Lord. Amen.

Lesson: James 5: 13 - 16

About anointing: (a brief statement to be made by the leader to remind all sharing in the act what it is about and where the emphasis must be placed)

Anointing is seen increasingly to be a sign of Biblical faithfulness and is understood to be a sacrament of Life. In the Bible there are two main emphases: anointing is indeed a sign of God's blessing upon an individual but it is also a sign of a person's submission to the sovereign will of God. It has to do with all that makes for wholeness within ourselves, within the community (Israel) and the church, and between the individual and God. It is found in a variety of settings and is used on a number of different occasions. Supremely it is a sign of Christ, God's Anointed One. He is the focus of the anointing, not the sick person; the action must affirm his presence, not dwell on the illness.

Confession of sin: (in silence but sharing any matters that should be brought out into the open)

Prayer: (may be spoken by the sick person and all the elders, or by the sick person alone)

Have mercy on me, O God, according to your unfailing love, according to your great compassion blot out my transgressions. Wash away all my iniquity and cleanse me from my sin. Amen

(Psalm 51:1,2)

Assurance of pardon: (may be spoken by someone acting as group leader, or by the whole group speaking together)

If we confess our sins, God is faithful and just
and will forgive us our sins
and purify us from all unrighteousness.

(1 John 1:9)

(spoken by the group leader)

Through the cross of Christ, God have mercy on you,
pardon you and set you free.
Know that you are forgiven and be at peace.
God strengthen you in all goodness
and keep you in eternal life. Amen.

Submission: (to be spoken by the person to be anointed but helpfully with the elders joining in)

I am no longer my own, but yours. Put me to what you will, rank me with whom you will; put me to doing, put me to suffering; let me be employed for you or laid aside for you, exalted for you or brought low for you; let me be full, let me be empty; let me have all things, let me have nothing; I freely and wholeheartedly yield all things to your good pleasure and disposal. And now, glorious and blessed God, Father, Son, and Holy Spirit, you are mine and I am yours. So be it. And the covenant now made on earth, let it be ratified in heaven. Amen.

(The Covenant Service of the Methodist Church)

Laying on of hands: (in which all the elders join, positively yet gently)

In the name of God most high, we lay our hands upon you.
Receive Christ's healing touch to make you whole
in body, mind and spirit.
The power of God strengthen you,
the love of God dwell in you,
and give you peace.

The anointing: (normally done by the group leader, using olive oil and making the sign of the cross on the forehead. Where appropriate the afflicted parts of the body may also be anointed)

> *I anoint you with this oil.*
> *May the power of the Saviour who suffered for you*
> *flow through your mind and body,*
> *lifting you to peace and inward strength.*
> *May he assure you of forgiveness*
> *and grant you healing. Amen.*

The Lord's Prayer: (gathering together the praise and thanksgiving offered in quietness or aloud by those present)

Parting prayer:

> *Be at peace!*
> *God be your comfort, your strength;*
> *God be your hope and support;*
> *God be your light and your way;*
> *and the blessing of God,*
> *Creator, Redeemer and Giver of Life,*
> *remain with you now and for ever. Amen.*

Further reading

Books

Booth, Howard	*Healing is Wholeness,* London, DSR Methodist Church and Churches' Council for Health and Healing, 1987
Carey, George	*The Church in the Market Place,* Eastbourne, Kingway Publications, 1989
Cormack, David	*Team Spirit,* London, Marc Europe, 1987
Coslett, Neil	*His Healing Hands,* Basingstoke, Marshall Pickering, 1985
Douglas, Tom	*Basic Groupwork,* London, Tavistock Publications, 1984
East, Reginald	*Heal the Sick,* London, Hodder and Stoughton, 1977
Grigor, Jean C	*Grow to Love,* Edinburgh, St Andrew's Press, 1977
Jacobs, Michael	*Swift to Hear,* London, SPCK, 1985
Long, Ann	*Listening,* London, Daybreak, 1990
MacDonald, Gordon	*Ordering Your Private World,* Crowborough, Highland Books, 1986
Maddocks, Morris	*The Christian Healing Ministry,* London, SPCK, 1981
Mallinson, John	*Building Small Groups,* Australia, Renewal Publications 1985
Matthew, Stewart & Lawson, Ken	*Caring for God's People,* Edinburgh, St Andrew's Press, 1989
Matthew, Stewart & Scott, Kenneth	*Leading God's People,* Edinburgh, St Andrew's Press, 1986
Newbigin, Lesslie	*The Good Shepherd,* Leighton Buzzard, The Faith Press, 1977

Oswald, Roy M & Leas, Speed B

> *The Inviting Church: a study in new member assimilation,*
> Washington, The Alban Institute Inc., 1987

Oswald, Roy M & McMakin

> *How to Prevent Lay Leader Burnout,* Washington, The Alban
> Institute Inc., 1986

Richards, John   *The Question of Healing Services,* London, Daybreak, 1989

Richards, John   *Understanding Anointing,* Shepperton, Middlesex, Renewal
                        Servicing, undated

Schaller, Lyle E   *Assimilating New Members,* Nashville, Abingdon Press, 1978

Wilkinson, John   *Health and Healing - studies in New Testament principles
                        and practice,* Edinburgh, The Handsel Press, 1980

Videos

Training in Eldership: Pastoral Care Church of Scotland, URC, Presbyterian Churches
   in Ireland and Wales- 45 minutes, covering 5 areas of eldership training:
   *Visiting in Happy Times, Visiting in Difficult Times, Handling a Grievance,
   Visiting on the Frontiers* and *Let's Pray.*
   (£25.00, but available on loan from denominational offices)

Training in Eldership Church of Scotland - 45 minutes, two programmes: *Vision
   on the Job;* and *Beyond the Doorstep.*
   (£25.00, or on loan from Church of Scotland)

Index

E

F

G

H

I

J